WAN Technologies
CCNA 4 Labs and Study Guide

W9-DIB-234

John Rullan

Cisco Press

800 East 96th Street
Indianapolis, Indiana 46240 USA

WAN Technologies

CCNA 4 Labs and Study Guide

John Rullan

Copyright© 2007 Cisco Systems, Inc.

Published by:
Cisco Press
800 East 96th Street
Indianapolis, IN 46240 USA

Printed in the United States of America 1 2 3 4 5 6 7 8 9 0

First Printing   August   2006

ISBN: 1-58713-173-0

Publisher
Paul Boger

Cisco Representative
Anthony Wolfenden

Cisco Press
Program Manager
Jeff Brady

Executive Editor
Mary Beth Ray

Managing Editor
Patrick Kanouse

Senior Development Editor
Christopher A. Cleveland

Senior Project Editor
San Dee Phillips

Copy Editor
Keith Cline

Technical Editor
Scott Empson

Team Coordinator
Vanessa Evans

Book and Cover Designer
Louisa Adair

Composition
Mark Shirar

Warning and Disclaimer

This book is designed to provide information about the labs for WAN Technologies CCNA 4 course of the Cisco Networking Academy Program. Every effort has been made to make this book as complete and as accurate as possible, but no warranty or fitness is implied.

The information is provided on an "as is" basis. The author, Cisco Press, and Cisco Systems, Inc. shall have neither liability nor responsibility to any person or entity with respect to any loss or damages arising from the information contained in this book or from the use of the discs or programs that may accompany it.

The opinions expressed in this book belong to the author and are not necessarily those of Cisco Systems, Inc.

Corporate and Government Sales

Cisco Press offers excellent discounts on this book when ordered in quantity for bulk purchases or special sales.

For more information please contact: U.S. Corporate and Government Sales 1-800-382-3419 corpsales@pearsontechgroup.com

For sales outside the U.S. please contact:
International Sales international@pearsoned.com

Feedback Information

At Cisco Press, our goal is to create in-depth technical books of the highest quality and value. Each book is crafted with care and precision, undergoing rigorous development that involves the unique expertise of members from the professional technical community.

Readers' feedback is a natural continuation of this process. If you have any comments regarding how we could improve the quality of this book, or otherwise alter it to better suit your needs, you can contact us through e-mail at feedback@ciscopress.com. Please make sure to include the book title and ISBN in your message.

We greatly appreciate your assistance.

Trademark Acknowledgments

All terms mentioned in this book that are known to be trademarks or service marks have been appropriately capitalized. Cisco Press or Cisco Systems, Inc. cannot attest to the accuracy of this information. Use of a term in this book should not be regarded as affecting the validity of any trademark or service mark.

CISCO SYSTEMS

Corporate Headquarters
Cisco Systems, Inc.
170 West Tasman Drive
San Jose, CA 95134-1706
USA
www.cisco.com
Tel: 408 526-4000
      800 553-NETS (6387)
Fax: 408 526-4100

European Headquarters
Cisco Systems International BV
Haarlerbergpark
Haarlerbergweg 13-19
1101 CH Amsterdam
The Netherlands
www-europe.cisco.com
Tel: 31 0 20 357 1000
Fax: 31 0 20 357 1100

Americas Headquarters
Cisco Systems, Inc.
170 West Tasman Drive
San Jose, CA 95134-1706
USA
www.cisco.com
Tel: 408 526-7660
Fax: 408 527-0883

Asia Pacific Headquarters
Cisco Systems, Inc.
Capital Tower
168 Robinson Road
#22-01 to #29-01
Singapore 068912
www.cisco.com
Tel: +65 6317 7777
Fax: +65 6317 7799

Cisco Systems has more than 200 offices in the following countries and regions. Addresses, phone numbers, and fax numbers are listed on the
Cisco.com Web site at www.cisco.com/go/offices.

Argentina • Australia • Austria • Belgium • Brazil • Bulgaria • Canada • Chile • China PRC • Colombia • Costa Rica • Croatia • Czech Republic
Denmark • Dubai, UAE • Finland • France • Germany • Greece • Hong Kong SAR • Hungary • India • Indonesia • Ireland • Israel • Italy
Japan • Korea • Luxembourg • Malaysia • Mexico • The Netherlands • New Zealand • Norway • Peru • Philippines • Poland • Portugal
Puerto Rico • Romania • Russia • Saudi Arabia • Scotland • Singapore • Slovakia • Slovenia • South Africa • Spain • Sweden
Switzerland • Taiwan • Thailand • Turkey • Ukraine • United Kingdom • United States • Venezuela • Vietnam • Zimbabwe

About the Author

John Rullan has been a teacher at Thomas Edison High School in Jamaica, New York, for the past 10 years and has been a Cisco instructor since 1998. He is the New York City Department of Education city-wide Cisco trainer and is the regional manager for Queens, New York, high schools. John also has taught CCNA, CCNP, and network security at the Borough of Manhattan Community College since 2000. He provides support to the academy community, working with the CCNA/CCNP Instructional Support team, too. John holds the Network+, CCNA, CCNP, and CCAI certifications.

About the Contributer

Jim Lorenz is a curriculum developer for the Cisco Networking Academy Program who co-authored the third editions of the Lab Companions for the CCNA courses. He has more than 20 years experience in information systems and has held various IT positions in several Fortune 500 companies, including Allied-Signal, Honeywell, and Motorola. Jim has developed and taught computer and networking courses for both public and private institutions for more than 15 years.

About the Technical Reviewer

Scott Empson, CCDA, CCNP, CCAI, Network+, is an instructor in the telecommunications department at the Northern Alberta Institute of Technology in Edmonton, Alberta, Canada. He teaches Cisco routing, switching, and network design courses to students at the post-secondary level. Scott holds three undergraduate degrees: a bachelor of arts, with a major in English; a bachelor of education, with a major in English/language arts; and a bachelor of applied information systems technology, with a major in network management.

Dedication

To my daughters, Brianna and Gabriella.

Acknowledgments

This book could not have been completed without hard work and dedication from my students at Thomas Edison High School. Their input and assistance in designing the challenge labs are what makes this book so special to be a part of. I want to give special thanks to Lourdes Luna, Charish Patel, Charles Chen, Alvar Lam, Nader Khandaker, Tulin Ravienthira, and Johanna Iniguez.

Contents at a Glance

Contents

Icons Used in This Book

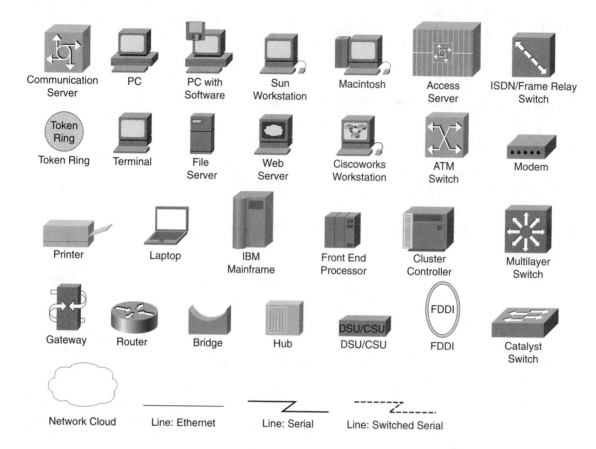

Command Syntax Conventions

The conventions used to present command syntax in this book are the same conventions used in the IOS Command Reference. The Command Reference describes these conventions as follows:

- **Bold** indicates commands and keywords that are entered literally as shown. In actual configuration examples and output (not general command syntax), bold indicates commands that are manually input by the user (such as a **show** command).

- *Italic* indicates arguments for which you supply actual values.

- Vertical bars (|) separate alternative, mutually exclusive elements.

- Square brackets ([ ]) indicate an optional element.

- Braces ({ }) indicate a required choice.

- Braces within brackets ([{ }]) indicate a required choice within an optional element.

Introduction

WAN Technologies CCNA 4 Labs and Study Guide is a supplement to your classroom and laboratory experience with the Cisco Networking Academy Program. Specifically, this book covers the fourth course of the CCNA curriculum. To succeed on the exam and achieve your CCNA certification, do everything in your power to arm yourself with a variety of tools and training materials to support your learning efforts. This *Labs and Study Guide* is just such a collection of tools. Used to its fullest extent, it will help you acquire the knowledge and practice the skills associated with the content area of v3.1.1 of the CCNA 4 WAN Technologies course. Specifically, this book helps you work on these main areas of CCNA 4:

- Network Address Translation
- Dynamic Host Configuration Protocol
- ISDN dialer maps and profiles
- Frame Relay

Goals and Methods

One of the goals of this book is to help you prepare for either the CCNA exam (640-801) or the ICND exam (640-811). Whether you are studying for the full exam or the second part of your CCNA, passing either of these exams means not only that you have the required knowledge of the technologies covered by the exam, but also that you can plan, design, implement, operate, and troubleshoot these technologies. In other words, these exams are rigorously application-based. In fact, if you view the main objectives for the CCNA exam at http://www.cisco.com/go/certifications, you will see the following four categories of objectives:

- Planning & Design
- Implementation & Operation
- Troubleshooting
- Technology

Although technology is listed last, a CCNA student cannot possibly plan, design, implement, operate, and troubleshoot networks without first fully grasping the technology. You should devote a significant amount of time and effort in the Study Guide section of each chapter to learning the concepts and theories before applying them in the Lab Exercises.

The **Study Guide** section offers exercises that help you learn the concepts and configurations crucial to your success as a CCNA exam candidate. Each chapter differs slightly and includes some or all of the following types of exercises:

- Vocabulary Matching and Completion
- Concept Questions
- Comprehensive Multiple-Choice Questions
- Internet Research

The **Lab Exercises** section includes all the online curriculum labs plus new comprehensive labs and challenge labs. The curriculum labs typically walk you through the configuration tasks step by step. The comprehensive labs combine many, if not all, of the configuration tasks of the curriculum labs without actually providing you with the commands. The challenge labs take this a step further, often giving you only a general requirement that you must implement fully without the details of each small step. In other words, you must use the knowledge and skills you gained in the curriculum labs from all four courses to successfully complete the comprehensive and challenge labs. In fact, you should not attempt the comprehensive or challenge labs until you have worked through all the Study Guide activities and the curriculum labs. Avoid the temptation to work through the comprehensive and challenge labs by flipping back through the curriculum labs when you are not sure of a command. Do not try to short-circuit your CCNA training. You need a deep understanding of CCNA knowledge and skills to ultimately succeed on the CCNA exam.

Who Should Read This Book?

This book should be read by students completing the final course of the CCNA curriculum. The challenge labs are designed to test your knowledge of and ability to configure and troubleshoot routing protocols, switching concepts, and WAN protocols. Based on the author's experience in the classroom, extensive practical knowledge is necessary to pass the CCNA certification.

Strategies for Exam Preparation

A successful CCNA certification candidate is knowledgeable about network design, implementation, and troubleshooting. Knowledge of theoretical terms and hands-on experience are both vital to successfully pass the certification.

How This Book Is Organized

Work through the **Study Guide** and **Lab Exercises** in the sequence they are presented. The sequence is designed to take you from a basic understanding of the knowledge through the full application and implementation of skills. Specifically, Chapters 1 through 6 and Appendix A include exerises and labs covering the following knowledge and skills:

Chapter 1, "Scaling IP Addresses," describes how to conserve IP addresses and how to communicate across the Internet and wide-area networks (WANs) that span the globe. The chapter goes over Network Address Translation (NAT) and Port Address Translation (PAT), two translation protocols for IP addresses, and Dynamic Host Configuration Protocol (DHCP), a method of auto-assigning IP addresses. The labs in this chapter explain how IP addresses are translated with NAT and PAT and the process of DHCP. They also cover the commands to configure both. A challenge lab tests your comprehension of the chapter.

Chapter 2, "WAN Technologies," introduces much of the terminology and general concepts encountered in a WAN. It lays the groundwork for an understanding of some of the more advanced concepts presented in later chapters. This chapter contains no labs, just exercises to reinforce your understanding of the terminology and concepts.

Chapter 3, "PPP," goes over the communication of individual links within the WAN that use certain types of encapsulation protocols. This chapter describes the High-Level Data Link Control (HDLC) protocol and the Point-to-Point Protocol (PPP). The challenge lab in this chapter tests your ability to configure PPP and any previous concepts you have learned thus far in this book.

Chapter 4, "ISDN and DDR," covers ISDN, a cost-effective, need-basis WAN technology that may substitute for a T1 connection or as just a step above a phone line. Dial-on-Demand Routing (DDR) is a method described in this chapter that makes ISDN cost-effective based on call setup and termination. The labs in this chapter test your knowledge of configuring dialer maps and dialer profiles.

Chapter 5, "Frame Relay," explains how Frame Relay, a packet-switched technology, connects local-area networks (LANs) across a cloud by using virtual circuits. The labs in this chapter give you a chance to configure basic Frame Relay, and two challenge labs test all the skills you have learned up to this point.

Chapter 6, "Introduction to Network Administration," describes basic network administration concepts. It also explains how to manage a network using different tools such as Simple Network Management Protocol (SNMP). Upon completion of the exercises in this chapter, students should better understand the different devices found on a LAN and the tools used to manage, test, and troubleshoot simple networks.

Appendix A, "WAN Troubleshooting, Questions and Lab Exercise," contains a practice challenge lab that tests your knowledge of all four courses of the CCNA curriculum. The lab exercise consists of a scenario that requires knowledge of troubleshooting methodologies.

Appendix B, "Adtran Configuration Lab," contains a step-by-step guide to configuring the Adtran Atlas 550.

Appendixes C, D, and E come into play within the curriculum labs. Where applicable, the curriculum lab tells you when to refer to these appendixes.

CHAPTER 1

Scaling IP Addresses

The Study Guide portion of this chapter uses a combination of matching, fill-in-the-blank, multiple-choice, and open-ended question exercises to test your knowledge of the theory of Network Address Translation (NAT), Port Address Translation (PAT), and Dynamic Host Configuration Protocol (DHCP).

The Lab Exercises portion of this chapter includes all the online curriculum labs and comprehensive labs and a challenge lab to ensure that you have mastered the practical, hands-on skills needed to configure NAT, Static NAT, PAT, and DHCP.

Study Guide

Scaling Networks with NAT and PAT

When connecting to the Internet, you must use a registered public IP address. When users connect to the Internet through a cable provider (such as Time Warner or Cablevision), the IP address assigned is registered and gives the user access to the Internet through the carrier's network. This arrangement actually makes the user's computer part of the cable provider's network. When you have more than one computer at home and each needs access to the Internet simultaneously, a router such as a Linksys usually does the trick. This device uses the single IP address assigned to you by your carrier and performs Port Address Translation (PAT), which allows multiple devices to access the Internet using a single unique address.

When it comes to a company, things are a little more complicated. Most companies require an entire network address for all their devices to access the Internet. Companies acquire these addresses from the American Registry of Internet Numbers (ARIN) or any Internet service provider (ISP) in their area. As the network grows, however, it might find that it no longer has enough addresses for all the devices. Instead of purchasing another network address (if even possible), another solution is to use Network Address Translation (NAT). Network administrators use private addresses put aside by RFC 1918 on the inside of their network. The router translates the device's inside private address into a registered global address each time the company needs to access the outside world. The use of NAT along with private addresses provides security by hiding a device's internal address from the outside world, thus making it difficult for "outsiders" to know exactly who is behind the device. Because not all devices inside a network need access to the Internet, NAT pools are created to determine who has access and who does not. Thus, NAT enables network administrators to allow multiple users to access the outside world dynamically; it also enables them to statically map an outside address to an internal device.

Concept Questions

1. Discuss the advantages of NAT.

_____

_____

_____

_____

2. RFC 1918 put aside three addresses and classified them as "private." Explain the difference between a public and private address.

_____

_____

_____

_____

3. When is it necessary to assign a static NAT address to a device inside your network? Give an example of a device, and explain the reason for doing so.

_____

_____

_____

_____

4. How many networks in total did RFC 1918 put aside?

_____

_____

_____

_____

5. Under what circumstances would you use NAT? PAT?

_____

_____

_____

_____

_____

_____

Research Assignment

This chapter discussed the difference between private and public addresses and their use within a network. Go to http://www.arin.net and research the following:

1. The American Registry for Internet Numbers (ARIN) allocates Internet number resources for the United States, Canada, and islands in the Caribbean and North Atlantic. What organization provides these same services in the following?

_____

a. Africa _____

b. Asia _____

c. Latin America _____

d. Europe, the Middle East, and Central Asia _____

2. How do you obtain a registered network number through ARIN?

_____

_____

_____

_____

3. List at least five items found on the IPv4 Network Request template provided by ARIN.

_____

_____

_____

_____

_____

4. What costs are associated with obtaining a 24-bit address from ARIN?

_____

_____

5. On the home page, click the "Who is" link. Enter a legitimate address in the Search box. This could be any address other than those put aside by RFC 1918. List five pieces of information you can retrieve about the owner of that address space.

_____

6. Enter **Cisco** in the "Who is" Search box. Describe some of the information that appears.

_____

_____

_____

Matching Terms

Match the definition on the left with the correct term on the right. Use each definition only one time.

Definitions

a. Uses a single IP address to support numerous inside local addresses

b. An IP address that is routable on the Internet

c. Addresses never to be assigned to an organization as a registered network number

d. An IP address assigned to a host in a private network

e. Identifies an interface that is on the private side of a network

f. Allows unregistered addresses to access the Internet using legitimate or public addresses

g. The IP address of a host on the outside of the network as it is known to the hosts on the inside network

h. A legitimate registered address that represents an inside local address to the outside world

i. Identifies an interface that is on the public side of the network

j. A one-to-one mapping of a public and private address

Terms

_____ inside local address

_____ NAT

_____ **ip nat outside** command

_____ outside local address

_____ static NAT

_____ inside global address

_____ Port Address Translation

_____ outside global address

_____ **ip nat inside** command

_____ RFC 1918

DHCP

Dynamic Host Configuration Protocol (DHCP) allows a device to dynamically receive network information upon boot. The basic information configured on a server includes network address, subnet mask, and default gateway. Domain Name System (DNS), NetBIOS, and Windows Internet Naming Service (WINS) server information are optional configurations if they exist on a network. As networks grow, DHCP deploys a plug-and-play design that allows new hosts to plug into the network without manual intervention. Designed by the Internet Engineering Task Force (IETF), it has become a standard component in network design and implementation.

Concept Questions

1. Explain the purpose of the DHCP **excluded-address** command.

   _____

   _____

   _____

2. Explain the advantages of DHCP over static allocation when a device such as a computer moves from one part of a network to another when multiple subnets exist.

   _____

   _____

   _____

3. Explain the difference between BOOTP and DHCP.

   _____

   _____

   _____

   _____

4. You are the network administrator of a company that uses DHCP on its network. Does DHCP provide a mechanism to prevent unauthorized users from plugging in and connecting to the network?

   _____

   _____

Matching Terms

Match the definition on the left with the correct term on the right. Use each definition only one time.

Definitions

a. A proposed configuration, from a DHCP server, that may include IP addresses, DNS server addresses, and lease time

b. A predecessor of DHCP (not dynamic)

c. A broadcast sent by a client to locate a DHCP server

d. Creates a pool with the specified name and puts the router in a specialized DHCP configuration mode

e. Configures the router to prohibit an individual address or range of addresses from being used when assigning addresses to clients

f. Verifies the operation of DHCP

g. A security server

h. Used to relay broadcast requests when the DHCP server resides on a different network than the host

i. A protocol used for assigning IP addresses to devices on a network (client/server mode)

j. DHCP assigning permanent IP addresses to the clients

Terms

_____ DHCP

_____ automatic allocation

_____ **show ip dhcp binding**

_____ TACACS server

_____ BOOTP

_____ **ip dhcp excluded-addresses**

_____ DHCPOFFER

_____ DHCPDISCOVER

_____ **ip dhcp pool word**

_____ **ip helper address**

Lab Exercises

Curriculum Lab 1-1: Configuring NAT (1.1.4a)

Figure 1-1   Topology for Lab 1-1

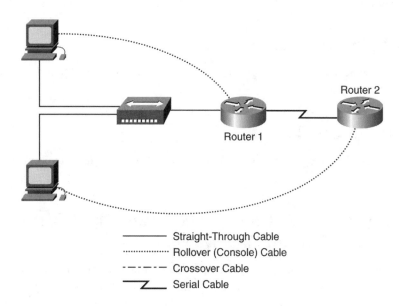

——————— Straight-Through Cable

····················· Rollover (Console) Cable

– – – – – Crossover Cable

⌐—Z— Serial Cable

Table 1-1   Lab Equipment Configuration

Router Designation	Router Name	Fast Ethernet 0 Address/Subnet Mask	Interface Type	Serial 0 Address/ Subnet Mask	Loopback 0 Address/Subnet Mask
Router 1	Gateway	10.10.10.1/24	DCE	200.2.2.18/30	—
Router 2	ISP	—	DTE	200.2.2.17/30	172.16.1.1/32

The enable secret password for both routers is **class**.

The enable, VTY, and console password for both routers is **cisco**.

Objective

- Configure a router to use NAT to convert internal IP addresses, which are typically private addresses, into outside public addresses.

Background/Preparation

The ISP has allocated the public classless interdomain routing (CIDR) IP address 199.99.9.32/27 to a company. This is equivalent to 30 public IP addresses. Because the company has an internal requirement for more than 30 addresses, the IT manager has decided to implement NAT. The company has decided to reserve the addresses 199.99.9.33 through 199.99.9.39 for static allocation and 199.99.9.40 through 199.99.9.62 for dynamic allocation. Routing between the ISP and the company's gateway router will be done using a static route from the ISP to the gateway and a default route from the gateway to the ISP. The ISP's connection to the Internet will be represented by a loopback address on the ISP router.

Cable a network that is similar to the one in Figure 1-1. You can use any router that meets the interface requirements in the diagram (that is, 800, 1600, 1700, 2500, and 2600 routers, or a combination). See the information in Appendix C, "Router Interface Summary Chart," to correctly specify the required interface identifiers based on the equipment in your lab. The configuration output in this lab results from 1721 series routers. Another router might produce slightly different output. Execute the following tasks on each router unless you are specifically instructed otherwise.

Start a HyperTerminal session.

See and implement the procedure documented in Appendix D, "Erasing and Reloading the Switch," before you continue with this lab.

Task 1: Configure the Routers

Configure the hostname, console, virtual terminal and enable passwords, and interfaces according to the chart.

Task 2: Save the Configuration

At the privileged EXEC mode prompt, on both routers, enter the command **copy running-config startup-config**.

Task 3: Configure the Hosts with the Proper IP Address, Subnet Mask, and Default Gateway

Each workstation should be able to ping the attached router. Troubleshoot as necessary. Hint: Remember to assign a specific IP address and default gateway to the workstation. If you are running Windows 98, check using **Start > Run > winipcfg**. If you are running Windows 2000 or later, check using **ipconfig** in a DOS window.

Task 4: Verify That the Network Is Functioning

Step 1.   From the attached hosts, ping the Fast Ethernet interface of the default gateway router.

Did the ping from the first host succeed? _____

Did the ping from the second host succeed? _____

Step 2.   If the answer is no for either question, troubleshoot the router and host configurations to find the error. Then, ping again until they succeed.

Task 5: Create a Static Route

Create a static route from the ISP to the gateway router. Addresses 199.99.9.32/27 have been allocated for Internet access outside the company. Use the **ip route** command to create the static route:

```
ISP(config)#ip route 199.99.9.32 255.255.255.224 200.2.2.18
```

Is the static route in the routing table? _____

What command checks the routing table contents?

_____

If the route was not in the routing table, give one reason why this might be so.

_____

Task 6: Create a Default Route

Step 1.   Add a default route, using the **ip route** command, from the gateway router to the ISP router. This forwards any unknown destination address traffic to the ISP:

```
Gateway(config)#ip route 0.0.0.0 0.0.0.0 200.2.2.17
```

Is the static route in the routing table? _____

Step 2.   Try to ping from one of the workstations to the ISP serial interface IP address.

Did the ping succeed? _____

Why?

_____

Task 7: Define the Pool of Usable Public IP Addresses

To define the pool of public addresses, use the **ip nat pool** command:

```
Gateway(config)#ip nat pool public_access 199.99.9.40 199.99.9.62 netmask 255.255.255.224
```

Task 8: Define an Access List That Matches the Inside Private IP Addresses

To define the access list to match the inside private addresses, use the **access-list** command:

```
Gateway(config)#access-list 1 permit 10.10.10.0 0.0.0.255
```

Task 9: Define the NAT Translation from Inside the List to Outside the Pool

To define the NAT, use the **ip nat inside source** command:

```
Gateway(config)#ip nat inside source list 1 pool public_access
```

Task 10: Specify the Interfaces

You must specify whether the active interfaces on the router are inside or outside interfaces with respect to NAT. To do this, use the **ip nat inside** or **ip nat outside** command:

```
Gateway(config)#interface fastethernet 0
Gateway(config-if)#ip nat inside
Gateway(config-if)#interface serial 0
Gateway(config-if)#ip nat outside
```

Task 11: Test the Configuration

Configure a workstation on the internal LAN with the IP address 10.10.10.10/24 and a default gateway 10.10.10.1. From the PC, ping 172.16.1.1. If successful, look at the NAT translation on the gateway router by using the command **show ip nat translations**.

What is the translation of the inside local host address?

_____

How is the inside global address assigned?

_____

How is the inside local address assigned?

_____

After you complete the previous tasks, log off (by entering **exit**) and turn the router off. Then remove and store the cables and adapter.

_____

_____

_____

_____

_____

_____

_____

_____

_____

_____

_____

_____

_____

_____

_____

_____

_____

_____

_____

_____

_____

_____

_____

_____

_____

_____

_____

_____

_____

_____

_____

_____

_____

_____

_____

_____

_____

_____

_____

_____

_____

_____

_____

_____

_____

Curriculum Lab 1-2: Configuring PAT (1.1.4b)

Figure 1-2   Topology for Lab 1-2

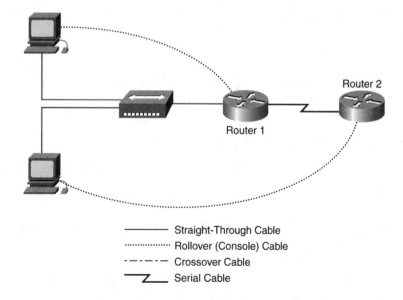

Table 1-2   Lab Equipment Configuration

Router Designation	Router Name	Fast Ethernet 0 Address/Subnet Mask	Interface Type	Serial 0 Address/Subnet Mask	Loopback 0 Address/Subnet Mask
Router 1	Gateway	10.10.10.1/24	DCE	200.2.2.18/30	—
Router 2	ISP	—	DTE	200.2.2.17/30	172.16.1.1/32

The enable secret password for both routers is **class**.

The enable, VTY, and console password for both routers is **cisco**.

Objective

- Configure a router to use PAT to convert internal IP addresses, which are typically private addresses, into outside public addresses.

Background/Preparation

Aidan McDonald has just received a Digital Subscriber Line (DSL) Internet connection in his home to a local ISP. The ISP has allocated only one IP address for use on the serial port of his remote-access device. Routing between the ISP and the home router will be achieved by using a static route between the ISP and gateway routers and a default route between the gateway and ISP routers. The ISP connection to the Internet is represented by a loopback address on the ISP router.

Cable a network that is similar to the one in Figure 1-2. You can use any router that meets the interface requirements in the diagram (that is, 800, 1600, 1700, 2500, and 2600 routers, or a combination). See the information in Appendix C to correctly specify the required interface identifiers based on the equipment in your lab. The configuration output in this lab results from 1721 series routers. Another router might produce slightly different output. Execute the following tasks on each router unless you are specifically instructed otherwise.

Start a HyperTerminal session.

See and implement the procedure documented in Appendix E, "Erasing and Reloading the Router," before you continue with this lab.

Task 1: Configure the Routers

Configure the hostname, console, virtual terminal and enable passwords, and interfaces according to the chart. If you have trouble doing this, see Lab 1-1, "Configuring NAT."

Task 2: Save the Configurations

At the privileged EXEC mode prompt on both routers, enter the command **copy running-config startup-config**.

Task 3: Configure the Hosts with the Proper IP Address, Subnet Mask, and Default Gateway

Each workstation should be able to ping the attached router. Troubleshoot as necessary. Hint: Remember to assign a specific IP address and default gateway to the workstation. If you are running Windows 98, check using **Start > Run > winipcfg**. If you are running Windows 2000 or later, check using **ipconfig** in a DOS window.

Task 4: Verify That the Network Is Functioning

Step 1.   From the attached hosts, ping the Fast Ethernet interface of the default gateway router.

Did the ping from the first host succeed? _____

Did the ping from the second host succeed? _____

Step 2.   If the answer is no for either question, troubleshoot the router and host configurations to find the error. Then, ping again until they succeed.

Task 5: Create a Default Route

Step 1.   Add a default route from the gateway to the ISP router. This forwards any unknown destination address traffic to the ISP. Use the **ip route** command to create the default route:

```
Gateway(config)#ip route 0.0.0.0 0.0.0.0 200.2.2.17
```

Is the route in the routing table? _____

Step 2.   Try to ping from one of the workstations to the ISP serial interface IP address.

Did the ping succeed? _____

Why?

_____

What command checks the routing table contents?

_____

Task 6: Define an Access List That Matches the Inside Private IP Addresses

To define the access list to match the inside private addresses, use the **access-list** command:

```
Gateway(config)#access-list 1 permit 10.10.10.0 0.0.0.255
```

Task 7: Define the PAT Translation from Inside the List to Outside the Address

To define the PAT translation, use the **ip nat inside source** command. This command with the **overload** option creates PAT by using the serial 0 IP address as the base:

```
Gateway(config)#ip nat inside source list 1 interface serial 0 overload
```

Task 8: Specify the Interfaces

You must specify whether the active interfaces on the router are inside or outside interfaces with respect to PAT (NAT). To do this, use the **ip nat inside** or **ip nat outside** command:

```
Gateway(config)#interface fastethernet 0
Gateway(config-if)#ip nat inside
Gateway(config-if)#interface serial 0
Gateway(config-if)#ip nat outside
```

Task 9: Test the Configuration

Configure a PC on the internal LAN with the IP address 10.10.10.10/24 and a default gateway 10.10.10.1. From the PCs, ping the Internet address 172.16.1.1. If successful, telnet to the same IP address. Then, look at the PAT translation on the gateway router by using the command **show ip nat translations**:

What is the translation of the inside local host addresses?

_____

_____

What does the number after the colon represent?

_____

Why do all the commands for PAT say NAT?

_____

After you complete the previous tasks, log off (by entering **exit**) and turn the router off. Then, remove and store the cables and adapter.

Curriculum Lab 1-3: Configuring Static NAT Addresses (1.1.4c)

Figure 1-3   Topology for Lab 1-3

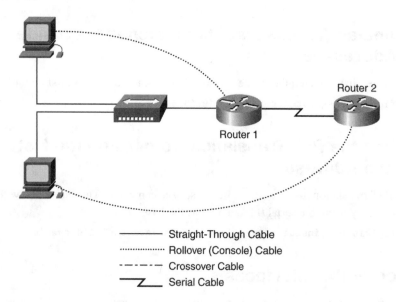

```
———————    Straight-Through Cable
·················    Rollover (Console) Cable
– – – –    Crossover Cable
—Z—    Serial Cable
```

Table 1-3   Lab Equipment Configuration

Router Designation	Router Name	Fast Ethernet 0 Address/Subnet Mask	Interface Type	Serial 0 Address/Subnet Mask	Loopback 0 Address/Subnet Mask
Router 1	Gateway	10.10.10.1/24	DCE	200.2.2.18/30	—
Router 2	ISP	—	DTE	200.2.2.17/30	172.16.1.1/32

The enable secret password for both routers is **class**.

The enable, VTY, and console password for both routers is **cisco**.

Objectives

- Configure a router to use NAT to convert internal IP addresses, which are typically private addresses, into outside public addresses.

- Configure static IP mapping to allow outside access to an internal PC.

Background/Preparation

The ISP has allocated the public CIDR IP address 199.99.9.32/27 to a company. This is equivalent to 30 public IP addresses. Because the company has an internal requirement for more than 30 addresses, the IT manager has decided to use NAT. The company has decided to reserve the addresses 199.99.9.33 through 199.99.9.39 for static allocation and 199.99.9.40 through 199.99.9.62 for dynamic allocation. Routing between the ISP and the gateway router will be done using a static route between the ISP and the gateway and a default route between the gateway and the ISP. The ISP connection to the Internet is represented by a loopback address on the ISP router.

Cable a network that is similar to the one in Figure 1-3. You can use any router that meets the interface requirements in the diagram (that is, 800, 1600, 1700, 2500, and 2600 routers, or a combination). See the information in Appendix C to correctly specify the required interface identifiers based on the equipment in your lab. The configuration output in this lab results from 1721 series routers. Another router might produce slightly different output. Execute the following tasks on each router unless you are specifically instructed otherwise.

Start a HyperTerminal session.

See and implement the procedure documented in Appendix E before you continue with this lab.

Task 1: Configure the Routers

Configure the hostname, console, virtual terminal and enable passwords, and interfaces according to the chart.

Task 2: Save the Configurations

At the privileged EXEC mode prompt on both routers, enter the command **copy running-config startup-config**.

Task 3: Configure the Hosts with the Proper IP Address, Subnet Mask, and Default Gateway

Each workstation should be able to ping the attached router. Troubleshoot as necessary. Hint: Remember to assign a specific IP address and default gateway to the workstation. If you are running Windows 98, check using **Start > Run > winipcfg**. If you are running Windows 2000 or later, check using **ipconfig** in a DOS window.

Task 4: Verify That the Network Is Functioning

Step 1.   From the attached hosts, ping the Fast Ethernet interface of the default gateway router.

Did the ping from the first host succeed? _____

Did the ping from the second host succeed? _____

Step 2.   If the answer is no for either question, troubleshoot the router and host configurations to find the error. Then, ping again until they succeed.

Task 5: Create a Static Route

Create a static route from the ISP to the gateway router. Addresses 199.99.9.32/27 have been allocated for Internet access outside the company. Use the **ip route** command to create the static route:

```
ISP(config)#ip route 199.99.9.32 255.255.255.224 200.2.2.18
```

Is the static route in the routing table? _____

What command checks the routing table contents? _____

If the route was not in the routing table, give one reason why this might be so. _____

Task 6: Create a Default Route

Step 1.   Add a default route, using the **ip route** command, from the gateway router to the ISP router. This forwards any unknown destination address traffic to the ISP:

```
Gateway(config)#ip route 0.0.0.0 0.0.0.0 200.2.2.17
```

Is the route in the routing table? _____

Step 2.   Try to ping from one of the workstations to the ISP serial interface IP address.

Did the **ping** succeed? _____

Why?

_____

Task 7: Define the Pool of Usable Public IP Addresses

To define the pool of public addresses, use the **ip nat pool** command:

```
Gateway(config)#ip nat pool public_access 199.99.9.40 199.99.9.62 netmask 255.255.255.224
```

Task 8: Define an Access List That Matches the Inside Private IP Addresses

To define the access list to match the inside private addresses, use the **access-list** command:

```
Gateway(config)#access-list 1 permit 10.10.10.0 0.0.0.255
```

Task 9: Define the NAT Translation from Inside the List to Outside the Pool

To define the NAT translation, use the **ip nat inside source** command:

```
Gateway(config)#ip nat inside source list 1 pool public_access
```

Task 10: Specify the Interfaces

You must specify whether the active interfaces on the router are inside or outside interfaces with respect to NAT. To do this, use either the **ip nat inside** or **ip nat outside** command.

Task 11: Configure Static Mapping

Step 1.   You should use workstation 1, 10.10.10.10/24, as the public WWW server. This server needs a permanent public IP address. Define this mapping by using a static NAT mapping.

Step 2.   Configure one of the PCs on the LAN with the IP address 10.10.10.10/24 and a default gateway 10.10.10.1. To configure a static IP NAT mapping, use the **ip nat inside source static** command at the privileged EXEC mode prompt:

```
Gateway(config)#ip nat inside source static 10.10.10.10 199.99.9.33
```

This permanently maps 199.99.9.33 to the inside address 10.10.10.10.

Step 3.   Look at the translation table:

```
Gateway#show ip nat translations
```

Does the mapping show up in the output of the **show** command? _____

Task 12: Test the Configuration

Step 1.   From the 10.10.10.10 workstation, ping 172.16.1.1.

Did the ping succeed? _____

Why? _____

Step 2.   From the ISP router, ping the host with the static NAT translation by entering **ping 10.10.10.10**.

What were the results of the ping? Did it succeed? _____

Why? _____

Step 3.   From the ISP router, ping 199.99.9.33. If successful, look at the NAT translation on the gateway router by using the command **show ip nat translations**.

What is the translation of the inside local host address?

_____

After you complete the previous tasks, log off (by entering **exit**) and turn the router off. Then, remove and store the cables and adapter.

Curriculum Lab 1-4: Verifying NAT and PAT Configuration (1.1.5)

Figure 1-4   Topology for Lab 1-4

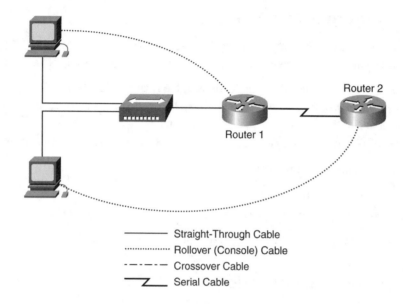

— Straight-Through Cable
············· Rollover (Console) Cable
– – – – – Crossover Cable
⟍Z⟍ Serial Cable

Table 1-4   Lab Equipment Configuration

Router Designation	Router Name	Fast Ethernet 0 Address/Subnet Mask	Interface Type	Serial 0 Address/Subnet Mask	Loopback 0 Address/Subnet Mask
Router 1	Gateway	10.10.10.1/24	DCE	200.2.2.18/30	—
Router 2	ISP	—	DTE	200.2.2.17/30	172.16.1.1/32

The enable secret password for both routers is **class**.

The enable, vty, and console password for both routers is **cisco**.

Objectives

- Configure a router for NAT and PAT.

- Test the configuration and verify NAT/PAT statistics.

Background/Preparation

The ISP has allocated the public CIDR IP address 199.99.9.32/30 to a company. This is equivalent to four public IP addresses. Because the company has an internal requirement for more than 30 addresses, the IT manager has decided to use NAT with PAT. Routing between the ISP and the gateway router will be done using a static route between the ISP and the gateway and a default route between the gateway and the ISP. The ISP connection to the Internet is represented by a loopback address on the ISP router.

Cable a network that is similar to the one in Figure 1-4. You can use any router that meets the interface requirements in the diagram (that is, 800, 1600, 1700, 2500, and 2600 routers, or a combination). See the information in Appendix C to correctly specify the required interface identifiers based on the equipment in your lab. The configuration output in this lab results from 1721 series routers. Another router might produce slightly different output. Execute the following tasks on each router unless you are specifically instructed otherwise.

Start a HyperTerminal session.

See and implement the procedure documented in Appendix E before you continue with this lab.

Task 1: Configure the Routers

Configure the hostname, console, virtual terminal and enable passwords, and interfaces according to the chart. If you have trouble doing this, see Lab 1-1, "Configuring NAT."

Task 2: Save the Configurations

At the privileged EXEC mode prompt on both routers, enter the command **copy running-config startup-config**.

Task 3: Configure the Hosts with the Proper IP Address, Subnet Mask, and Default Gateway

Each workstation should be able to ping the attached router. Troubleshoot as necessary. Hint: Remember to assign a specific IP address and default gateway to the workstation. If you are running Windows 98, check using **Start > Run > winipcfg**. If you are running Windows 2000 or later, check using **ipconfig** in a DOS window.

Task 4: Verify That the Network Is Functioning

Step 1.   From the attached hosts, ping the Fast Ethernet interface of the default gateway router.

Did the ping from the first host succeed? _____

Did the ping from the second host succeed? _____

Step 2.   If the answer is no for either question, troubleshoot the router and host configurations to find the error. Then, ping again until they succeed.

Task 5: Create a Static Route

Create a static route from the ISP to the gateway router. Addresses 199.99.9.32/27 have been allocated for Internet access outside the company. Use the **ip route** command to create the static route:

```
ISP(config)#ip route 199.99.9.32 255.255.255.252 200.2.2.18
```

Is the static route in the routing table? _____

What command checks the routing table contents? _____

If the route was not in the routing table, give one reason why this might be so. _____

Task 6: Create a Default Route

Step 1.   Add a default route, using the **ip route** command, from the gateway router to the ISP router. This forwards any unknown destination address traffic to the ISP:

```
Gateway(config)#ip route 0.0.0.0 0.0.0.0 200.2.2.17
```

Is the route in the routing table? _____

Step 2.   Try to ping from one of the workstations to the ISP serial interface IP address.

Did the ping succeed? _____

Why?

_____

Task 7: Define the Pool of Usable Public IP Addresses

To define the pool of public addresses, use the **ip nat pool** command:

```
Gateway(config)#ip nat pool public_access 199.99.9.32 199.99.9.35 netmask 255.255.255.252
```

Task 8: Define an Access List That Matches the Inside Private IP Addresses

To define the access list to match the inside private addresses, use the **access-list** command:

```
Gateway(config)#access-list 1 permit 10.10.10.0 0.0.0.255
```

Task 9: Define the NAT Translation from Inside the List to Outside the Pool

To define the NAT translation, use the **ip nat inside source** command:

```
Gateway(config)#ip nat inside source list 1 pool public_access overload
```

Task 10: Specify the Interfaces

You must specify whether the active interfaces on the router are inside or outside interfaces with respect to NAT. To do this, use the **ip nat inside** or **ip nat outside** command:

```
Gateway(config)#interface fastethernet 0
Gateway(config-if)#ip nat inside
Gateway(config-if)#interface serial 0
Gateway(config-if)#ip nat outside
```

Task 11: Test the Configuration

From the workstations, ping 172.16.1.1. Open multiple DOS windows on each workstation and telnet to the 172.16.1.1 address. Next, view the NAT translations on the gateway router with the command **show ip nat trans**.

_____

_____

_____

_____

_____

What is the translation of the inside local host addresses?

_____

_____

Task 12: Verify NAT/PAT Statistics

To view the NAT and PAT statistics, enter the **show ip nat statistics** command at the privileged EXEC mode prompt.

_____

_____

_____

_____

_____

_____

_____

_____

_____

_____

_____

_____

_____

_____

_____

_____

How many active translations have taken place? _____

How many addresses are in the pool? _____

How many addresses have been allocated so far? _____

After you complete the previous tasks, log off (by entering **exit**) and turn the router off. Then, remove and store the cables and adapter.

Curriculum Lab 1-5: Troubleshooting NAT and PAT (1.1.6)

Figure 1-5   Topology for Lab 1-5

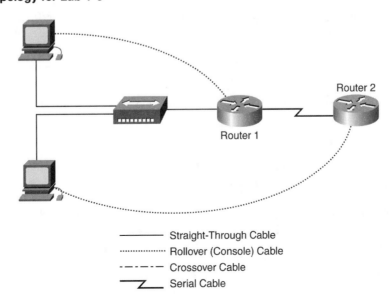

    ────────── Straight-Through Cable
    ················ Rollover (Console) Cable
    ─ ─ ─ ─ ─ Crossover Cable
    ─────Z─── Serial Cable

Table 1-5   Lab Equipment Configuration

Router Designation	Router Name	Fast Ethernet 0 Address/Subnet Mask	Interface Type	Serial 0 Address/ Subnet Mask	Loopback 0 Address/Subnet Mask
Router 1	Gateway	10.10.10.1/24	DCE	200.2.2.18/30	—
Router 2	ISP	—	DTE	200.2.2.17/30	172.16.1.1/32

The enable secret password for both routers is **class**.

The enable, VTY, and console password for both routers is **cisco**.

Objectives

- Configure a router for NAT and PAT.

- Troubleshoot NAT and PAT by using **debug**.

Background/Preparation

The ISP has allocated the public CIDR IP address 199.99.9.32/30 to a company. This is equivalent to four public IP addresses. Because the company has an internal requirement for more than 30 addresses, the IT manager has decided to use NAT and PAT. Routing between the ISP and the gateway router will be done using a static route between the ISP and the gateway and a default route between the gateway and the ISP. The ISP's connection to the Internet is represented by a loopback address on the ISP router.

Cable a network that is similar to the one in Figure 1-5. You can use any router that meets the interface requirements in the diagram (that is, 800, 1600, 1700, 2500, and 2600 routers, or a combination). See the information in Appendix C to correctly specify the required interface identifiers based on the equipment in your lab. The configuration output in this lab results from 1721 series routers. Another router might produce slightly different output. Execute the following tasks on each router unless you are specifically instructed otherwise.

Start a HyperTerminal session.

See the erase and reload instructions in Appendix E. Perform those tasks on all routers in this lab assignment before you continue.

Task 1: Configure the Routers

Configure the hostname, console, virtual terminal and enable passwords, and interfaces according to the chart. If you have trouble doing this, see Lab 1-1, "Configuring NAT."

Task 2: Save the Configurations

At the privileged EXEC mode prompt on both routers, enter the command **copy running-config startup-config**.

Task 3: Configure the Hosts with the Proper IP Address, Subnet Mask, and Default Gateway

Each workstation should be able to ping the attached router. Troubleshoot as necessary. Hint: Remember to assign a specific IP address and default gateway to the workstation. If you are running Windows 98, check using **Start > Run > winipcfg**. If you are running Windows 2000 or later, check using **ipconfig** in a DOS window.

Task 4: Verify That the Network Is Functioning

Step 1. From the attached hosts, ping the Fast Ethernet interface of the default gateway router.

Did the ping from the first host succeed? _____

Did the ping from the second host succeed? _____

Step 2. If the answer is no for either question, troubleshoot the router and host configurations to find the error. Then, ping again until they succeed.

Task 5: Create a Static Route

Create a static route from the ISP to the gateway router. Addresses 199.99.9.32/27 have been allocated for Internet access outside the company. Use the **ip route** command to create the static route:

```
ISP(config)#ip route 199.99.9.32 255.255.255.252 200.2.2.18
```

Is the static route in the routing table? _____

What command checks the routing table contents? _____

If the route was not in the routing table, give one reason why this might be so. _____

Task 6: Create a Default Route

Step 1. Add a default route, using the **ip route** command, from the gateway router to the ISP router. This forwards any unknown destination address traffic to the ISP:

```
Gateway(config)#ip route 0.0.0.0 0.0.0.0 200.2.2.17
```

Is the route in the routing table? _____

Step 2. Try to ping from one of the workstations to the ISP serial interface IP address.

Did the ping succeed? _____

Why?

Task 7: Define the Pool of Usable Public IP Addresses

To define the pool of public addresses, use the **ip nat pool** command:

```
Gateway(config)#ip nat pool public_access 199.99.9.32 199.99.9.35 netmask 255.255.255.252
```

Task 8: Define an Access List That Matches the Inside Private IP Addresses

To define the access list to match the inside private addresses, use the **access-list** command:

```
Gateway(config)#access-list 1 permit 10.10.10.0 0.0.0.255
```

Task 9: Define the NAT Translation from Inside the List to Outside the Pool

To define the NAT translation, use the **ip nat inside source** command:

```
Gateway(config)#ip nat inside source list 1 pool public_access overload
```

Task 10: Specify the Interfaces

You must specify whether the active interfaces on the router are inside or outside interfaces with respect to NAT. To do this, use the **ip nat inside** command:

```
Gateway(config)#interface fastethernet 0
Gateway(config-if)#ip nat inside
```

Task 11: Test the Configuration

Step 1.   Turn on debugging for the NAT process by entering **debug ip nat** at the privileged EXEC mode prompt.

Does the **debug** command show output? _____

Step 2.   If translation were taking place, there would be output from the **debug** command. In reviewing the running configuration of the gateway router, you see that the **ip nat outside** statement has not been entered on the serial 0 interface. To configure this, enter the following:

```
Gateway(config)#interface serial 0
Gateway(config-if)#ip nat outside
```

Step 3.   From the workstations, ping 172.16.1.1.

If you entered the **ip nat outside** statement correctly, there should be output from the **debug ip nat** command.

What does NAT*: S=10.10.10.? -> 199.99.9 mean?

_____

Step 4.   Stop the **debug** output by entering **undebug all** at the privileged EXEC mode prompt.

After you complete the previous tasks, log off (by entering **exit**) and turn the router off. Then, remove and store the cables and adapter.

Curriculum Lab 1-6: Configuring DHCP (1.2.6)

Figure 1-6   Topology for Lab 1-6

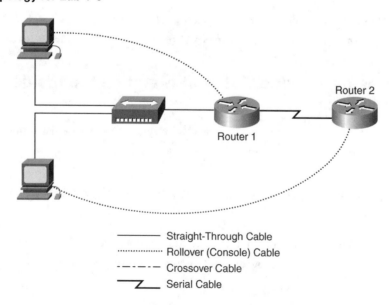

Straight-Through Cable

Rollover (Console) Cable

Crossover Cable

Serial Cable

Table 11-6   Lab Equipment Configuration

Router Designation	Router Name	Fast Ethernet 0 Address/Subnet Mask	Interface Type	Serial 0 Address/ Subnet Mask	Loopback 0 Address/Subnet Mask
Router 1	campus	172.16.12.1/24	DCE	172.16.1.6/30	—
Router 2	ISP	—	DTE	172.16.1.5/30	172.16.13.1/32

The enable secret password for both routers is **class**.

The enable, VTY, and console password for both routers is **cisco**.

Objective

■ Configure a router for DHCP to dynamically assign addresses to attached hosts.

Background/Preparation

Routing between the ISP and the campus router is by way of a static route between the ISP and the gateway and a default route between the gateway and the ISP. The ISP connection to the Internet is identified by a loopback address on the ISP router.

Cable a network that is similar to the one in Figure 1-6. You can use any router that meets the interface requirements in the diagram (that is, 800, 1600, 1700, 2500, and 2600 routers, or a combination). See the information in Appendix C to correctly specify the required interface identifiers based on the equipment in your lab. The configuration output in this lab results from 1721 series routers. Another router might produce slightly different output. Execute the following tasks on each router unless you are specifically instructed otherwise.

Start a HyperTerminal session.

See and implement the procedure documented in Appendix E before you continue with this lab.

Task 1: Configure the Routers

Configure the hostname, console, virtual terminal and enable passwords, and interfaces according to the chart. If you have trouble doing this, see Lab 1-1, "Configuring NAT."

Task 2: Save the Configurations

At the privileged EXEC mode prompt on both routers, enter the command **copy running-config startup-config**.

Task 3: Create a Static Route

Addresses 172.16.12.0/24 have been allocated for Internet access outside the company. Use the **ip route** command to create the static route:

```
ISP(config)#ip route 172.16.12.0 255.255.255.0 172.16.1.6
```

Is the static route in the routing table? _____

Task 4: Create a Default Route

Use the **ip route** command to add a default route from the campus router to the ISP router. This provides the mechanism to forward unknown destination address traffic to the ISP:

```
campus(config)#ip route 0.0.0.0 0.0.0.0 172.16.1.5
```

Is the route in the routing table? _____

Task 5: Create the DHCP Address Pool

To configure the campus LAN pool, use the following commands:

```
campus(config)#ip dhcp pool campus
campus(dhcp-config)#network 172.16.12.0 255.255.255.0
campus(dhcp-config)#default-router 172.16.12.1
campus(dhcp-config)#dns-server 172.16.1.2
campus(dhcp-config)#domain-name foo.com
campus(dhcp-config)#netbios-name-server 172.16.1.10
```

Task 6: Exclude Addresses from the Pool

To exclude addresses from the pool, use the following command:

```
campus(dhcp-config)#ip dhcp excluded-address 172.16.12.1 172.16.12.10
```

Task 7: Verify DHCP Operation

Step 1.   At each workstation on the directly connected subnet, configure the TCP/IP properties so that the workstation obtains an IP address and DNS server address from the DHCP server (see Figure 1-7). After you change and save the configuration, reboot the workstation.

Figure 1-7   TCP/IP Properties Dialog Box

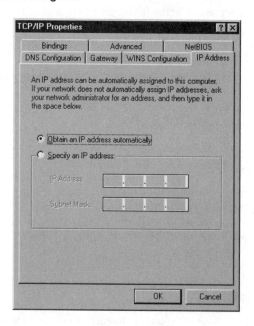

Step 2.   To confirm the TCP/IP configuration information on each host, use **Start > Run > winipcfg**. If you are running Windows 2000, check using **ipconfig** in a DOS window.

What IP address was assigned to the workstation?

_____

What other information was assigned automatically?

_____

When was the lease obtained?

_____

When will the lease expire?

_____

Task 8: View DHCP Bindings

From the campus router, you can see the bindings for the hosts. To see the bindings, use the command **show ip dhcp binding** at the privileged EXEC mode prompt.

_____

_____

_____

_____

What IP addresses were assigned?

_____

What three other fields does the output list?

_____

After you complete the previous tasks, log off (by entering **exit**) and turn the router off. Then, remove and store the cables and adapter.

Curriculum Lab 1-7: Configuring DHCP Relay (1.2.8)

Figure 1-8   Topology for Lab 1-7

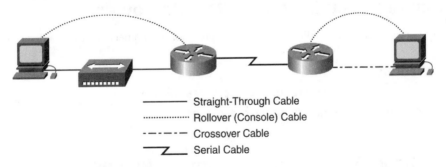

——————— Straight-Through Cable
·············· Rollover (Console) Cable
–·—·–·— Crossover Cable
——Z—— Serial Cable

Table 1-7   Lab Equipment Configuration

Router Designation	Router Name	Fast Ethernet 0 Address/Subnet Mask	Interface Type	Serial 0 Address
Router 1	campus	172.16.12.1/24	DCE	172.16.1.6/30
Router 2	remote	172.16.13.1/24	DTE	172.16.1.5/30

The enable secret password for both routers is **class**.

The enable, VTY, and console password for both routers is **cisco**.

Objectives

- Configure a router for DHCP.

- Add the capability for workstations to remotely obtain DHCP addresses and dynamically assign addresses to the attached hosts.

Background/Preparation

A DHCP client uses IP broadcasts to find the DHCP server. However, routers do not forward these broadcasts, so in the case of the remote LAN, the workstations cannot locate the DHCP server. The router must be configured with the **ip helper-address** command to enable forwarding of these broadcasts, as unicast packets, to the specific server.

Routing between the remote and the campus router is done by using a static route between remote and gateway and a default route between gateway and remote.

Cable a network that is similar to the one in Figure 1-8. You can use any router that meets the interface requirements in the diagram (that is, 800, 1600, 1700, 2500, and 2600 routers, or a combination). See the information in Appendix C to correctly specify the required interface identifiers based on the equipment in your lab. The configuration output in this lab results from 1721 series routers. Another router might produce slightly different output. Execute the following tasks on each router unless you are specifically instructed otherwise.

Start a HyperTerminal session.

See and implement the procedure documented in Appendix E before you continue with this lab.

Task 1: Configure the Routers

Configure the hostname, console, virtual terminal and enable passwords, and interfaces according to the chart. If you have a problem completing this, see Lab 1-1, "Configuring NAT."

Task 2: Configure Routing on the Remote Router

Using Open Shortest Path First (OSPF) as the routing protocol, set up network as area 0 and the process ID as 1:

```
remote(config)#router ospf 1
remote(config-router)#network 172.16.1.0 0.0.0.255 area 0
remote(config-router)#network 172.16.13.0 0.0.0.255 area 0
```

Task 3: Configure Routing on the Campus Router

Using OSPF as the routing protocol, set up the network as area 0 and the process ID as 1:

```
campus(config)#router ospf 1
campus(config-router)#network 172.16.1.0 0.0.0.255 area 0
campus(config-router)#network 172.16.12.0 0.0.0.255 area 0
```

Do OSPF routes exist in the routing table? _____

Task 4: Save the Configurations

At the privileged EXEC mode prompt on both routers, enter the command **copy running-config startup-config**.

Task 5: Create the Campus DHCP Address Pool on the Campus Router

To configure the campus LAN pool, use the following commands:

```
campus(config)#ip dhcp pool campus
campus(dhcp-config)#network 172.16.12.0 255.255.255.0
campus(dhcp-config)#default-router 172.16.12.1
campus(dhcp-config)#dns-server 172.16.12.2
campus(dhcp-config)#domain-name foo.com
campus(dhcp-config)#netbios-name-server 172.16.12.10
```

Task 6: Create the Remote DHCP Address Pool on the Campus Router

To configure the remote LAN pool, use the following commands:

```
campus(dhcp-config)#ip dhcp pool remote
campus(dhcp-config)#network 172.16.13.0 255.255.255.0
campus(dhcp-config)#default-router 172.16.13.1
campus(dhcp-config)#dns-server 172.16.12.2
campus(dhcp-config)#domain-name foo.com
campus(dhcp-config)#netbios-name-server 172.16.12.10
```

Task 7: Exclude Addresses from the Pool

To exclude addresses from the pool, use the following commands:

```
campus(dhcp-config)#ip dhcp excluded-address 172.16.12.1 172.16.12.10
campus(dhcp-config)#ip dhcp excluded-address 172.16.13.1 172.16.13.10
```

This defines the address range that the DHCP server excludes from dynamic issue.

Why would addresses be excluded?

Task 8. Verify DHCP Operation on the Campus Router

Step 1.   From the workstation directly connected to the campus router, configure the TCP/IP properties for the workstation to obtain its IP properties automatically from DHCP. These properties include the IP and DNS server address (see Figure 1-9).

Figure 1-9   TCP/IP Properties Dialog Box

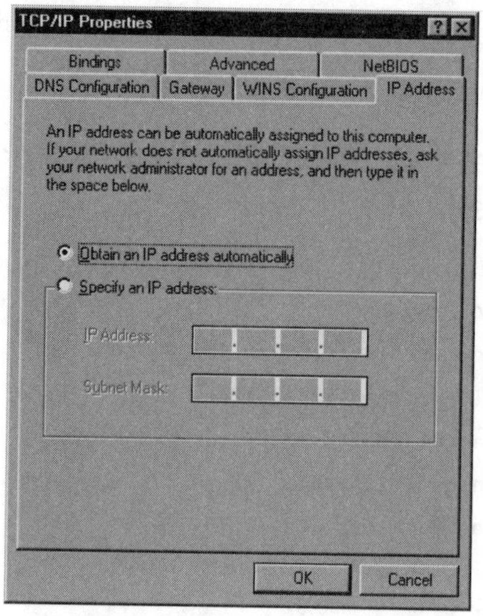

Step 2.   After you change the configuration, reboot the workstation. View the TCP/IP configuration information. If you are running Windows 98, go to **Start > Run > winipcfg**. With Windows 2000 or higher, use **ipconfig** in a DOS window.

What IP address was assigned to the workstation? _____

Task 9: Verify DHCP Operation on the Remote Router

Repeat Task 8 using the workstation that is attached to the remote router.

Is a valid address assigned from the DHCP pool? _____

What IP address was assigned to the workstation?

_____

What does this address (if any) represent?

_____

_____

Task 10: Configure DHCP Relay

Configure the remote router with the **ip helper-address** command to enable forwarding of broadcasts, as unicast packets, to the specific server. You must configure this command on the LAN interface of the remote router for DHCP to function:

```
remote(config)#interface fastethernet 0
remote(config-if)#ip helper-address 172.16.12.1
```

Task 11: Verify DHCP Operation on the Remote Router

Step 1. Reboot the workstation that is attached to the remote router.

Is a valid address assigned from the DHCP pool? _____

What IP address was assigned to the workstation? _____

Step 2. If there is no IP address, troubleshoot the workstation and router configurations and repeat Task 11.

Task 12: View DHCP Bindings

From the campus router, you can see the bindings for the hosts. To see the bindings, use the command **show ip dhcp binding** at the privileged EXEC mode prompt.

Which IP addresses are assigned to the hosts?

_____

After you complete the previous tasks, log off (by entering **exit**) and turn the router off. Then, remove and store the cables and adapter.

Comprehensive Lab 1-8: Configuring NAT, PAT, and Static NAT

You are the network administrator of ACME, a start-up marketing company with a limited number of users. Your company purchased a small range of public addresses from your ISP for global communication. Your company's IP address is 200.127.54.0/26—which is the equivalent of 62 assignable addresses. Routing between ACME and the ISP is accomplished using a classless routing protocol. A loopback address represents the ISP's connection to the Internet. Figure 1-10 shows the network topology for this lab.

Figure 1-10   Network Topology for Lab 1-8

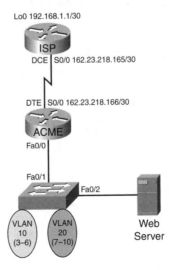

Objective

- Configure a router with multiple NAT pools to accommodate numerous VLANs within the network. To complete this lab, you can use 2620, 1721, and 1760 routers and 2950 switches.

Configuration Tasks

- Cable and configure the equipment according to the topology diagram in Figure 1-10.

- Control access to the console port on all devices using **cisco** as the password.

- Use an encrypted password when accessing the privileged mode of all devices using **class** as the password.

- Restrict remote access to all devices using **itsasecret** as the password.

- Configure interface descriptions.

Addressing Scheme

- As the network administrator of ACME, you decide to use the 192.168 100.0 /24 address for devices inside your network.

- You must create an addressing scheme that will support three subnets:

    - Department of Information Services (DIS) Department: 12 users

    - Finance department: 13 users

    - Marketing department: 30 users

VLANs

- Create three VLANs and apply them to the following ports on the ALswitch:

    - VLAN 1: DIS.

    - VLAN 10: Marketing department ports 3–6.

    - VLAN 20: Finance department ports 7–10.

    - All unassigned ports should be assigned to VLAN 1. If they are unused, they should be disabled for security purposes.

- Configure trunk ports as indicated by the diagram. All trunk links should carry traffic for all VLANs.

- Configure the switch with an address from VLAN 1 with an appropriate default gateway.

- Configure inter-VLAN routing on the ACME router using IEEE 802.1q encapsulation.

Web Server

- Configure the web server with an address from VLAN 1.

NAT

Using the public addresses assigned to you by the ISP, configure three separate NAT pools for each of the following:

- You are to allow all 30 users in the Marketing department to access the Internet by pulling an IP address dynamically (NAT).

- Users in the Finance department will communicate with the outside world using the same IP address (PAT).

- The company's web server is inside the private network and must be statically assigned a public address.

Routing

- Use a classless routing protocol to route traffic between the ISP and ACME routers. Because you are the network administrator, you decide which protocol to use.

Challenge Lab 1-9: NAT, PAT, DHCP

Estimated time: 90 minutes

Figure 1-11   Network Topology for Lab 1-9

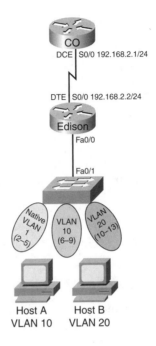

Note

This lab tests your knowledge of NAT, PAT, DHCP, static, and default routes. It builds on VLAN concepts and configurations you have learned previously in CCNA 3 of the curriculum. You might find it useful to review notes and labs from CCNA 3 before proceeding.

General Configuration Tasks

- Cable and configure the equipment based on the topology shown in Figure 1-11.

- Control access to the console on all devices using **cisco** as the password.

- Use an encrypted password when accessing the privileged mode of all devices using **class** as the password.

- Restrict remote access to all devices using **itsasecret** as the password.

- Configure descriptions on all interfaces.

Addressing

- As the network administrator, you decide which private address to use on the inside of your network. Choose a Class B address with a 24-bit mask from RFC 1918.

- Use the address that you have chosen and create three subnets to accommodate users on the management, teacher, and student VLANs:

  - 90 users on the student VLAN

  - 20 users on the teacher VLAN

  - 12 users on the management VLAN

VLANs

- Create three VLANs and apply them to the following ports on the ALswitch:

    - VLAN 1: Management VLAN ports 2–5

    - VLAN 10: Student VLAN ports 6–9

    - VLAN 20: Teacher VLAN ports 10–13

- Configure trunk ports as indicated in the diagram. All trunk links should carry traffic for all VLANs.

- Configure the switch with an address from VLAN 1 with the appropriate default gateway.

- Configure inter-VLAN routing on the Edison router using IEEE 802.1q encapsulation.

Static Routes

- Create a default route on the Edison router so that the hosts can access all networks on the Central Office router.

- Create a static route on the Central Office router so that it can connect to all networks on the Edison LAN.

DHCP

- Instead of assigning a static IP address to each device on the network, use DHCP to assign IP addresses to all devices on the student VLAN.

- Configure the appropriate default gateway and exclude the first 10 addresses from this pool.

- Connect the PCs to the appropriate switch ports as indicated by the diagram. Verify that the PCs on the student VLAN have been assigned an address from the correct subnet pool.

- Devices on the teacher VLAN will be statically assigned. Remember to use only those addresses suitable for teacher client devices.

NAT/PAT

- Only traffic from the student and teacher VLANs will be NATed when leaving the Edison router. Traffic from the management VLAN will remain the same.

- The NAT/PAT pools should be created from the unused address space on the WAN subnet between the Central Office and Edison routers. Separate pools should be created for each VLAN.

- Create a large pool for students so that they are each assigned a unique address when crossing the WAN.

- All devices on the teacher VLAN will cross the WAN as the same address. In other words, the teacher pool will require overloading (PAT).

Testing and Verification

- Test connectivity between PCs, to the default gateway, and from the PC to the loopback interface on the Central Office router.

- Ensure that devices on the student VLAN have an address assigned from the DHCP pool.

- Ensure that each device on the student VLAN crosses the WAN link with an address from the NAT pool and that each device on the teacher VLAN crosses the WAN with the same address assigned in that pool.

Reflection

List five commands other than the **show running-config command** that you used to verify the correct configuration of the lab assignment. Explain how each command proved useful in completing this lab.

Challenge Lab 1-10: Double NAT Configuration

Figure 1-12   Topology for Challenge Lab 1-10

This lab requires you to perform NAT on two different routers. The Scissor LAN addresses are translated on the Scissor router using remaining address space from the WAN connection and are translated again on the Paper router using a different set of addresses.

Objectives

- Configure VLANs and inter-VLAN routing.
- Configure DHCP.
- Configure NAT and PAT.
- Configure RIPv2.

Task 1: Cabling and Configuration

Cable and configure equipment according to the diagram in Figure 1-12.

Task 2: IP Addressing

Assign IP addresses on your routers using the appropriate addressing scheme for each LAN based on the detailed VLAN information in Figure 1-12. This task tests your knowledge of Classless Interdomain Routing (CIDR) and Variable-Length subnet Masks (VLSMs).

Task 3: Inter-VLAN Communication

Configure inter-VLAN routing using IEEE 802.1q encapsulation.

Task 4: Configure VLANs, VLAN Ports, and the HTTP Server

Step 1.   Configure the Scissor switch and the Paper switch with the following VLANs:

- VLAN 1
- VLAN 10: Wholesale
- VLAN 20: Retail

Step 2.   Assign the VLANs to the appropriate ports:

- VLAN 1: All unassigned ports
- VLAN 10: Ports 6–10
- VLAN 20: Ports 11–15

Step 3.   Set up the Rock router as an HTTP server.

Task 5: Configure and Verify RIPv2 Operation

Step 1.   Configure RIPv2 on each router and advertise all directly connected networks.

Step 2.   Verify functionality with the **show ip route** command.

Task 6: Configure DHCP

Step 1.   Configure DHCP on the Paper and Scissor routers.

Step 2.   Exclude the first 10 addresses from each VLAN.

Task 7: Configure NAT and PAT

Step 1.   Configure NAT and PAT on the Paper and Scissor routers.

Step 2.   Translate the Scissor LAN with the unused address space from 196.100.10.0/24 in this way:

■ VLAN 1 will access the outside world using one IP address.

■ Create a NAT pool for VLAN 10.

■ Create a NAT pool for VLAN 20.

Step 3.   All addresses will be retranslated at the Paper router when communicating with the Rock router in the following way:

■ All Scissor addresses will use the 24.58.96.253/30 address.

■ The Paper LAN will use the 24.58.96.254/30 address.

Task 8: Verify Configurations

Verify configurations using the appropriate commands.

Hosts on the Scissor LAN should ping the Paper LAN using an address from the 196.100.10.0/24 network.

Hosts on the Scissor LAN should ping the Rock router using the 24.58.96.253/30 address.

Hosts on the Paper LAN should ping the Scissor LAN using an address from the 192.168.20.0/23 network.

Hosts on the Paper LAN should ping the Rock router using the 24.58.96.254/30 address.

Optional Lab 1-11: Using a Linksys Router to Simulate a Home Network

In this lab, you use a Linksys router to simulate a real-world example of a home network.

Figure 1-13   Network Topology for Lab 1-11

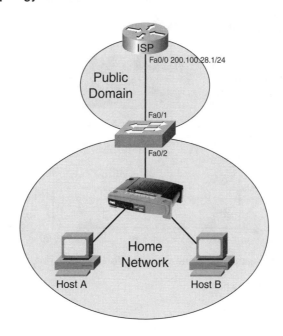

Equipment

■ You can complete this lab using any Linksys router other than voice-enabled models. You can use 1700, 2500, and 2600 series routers for this lab to simulate the ISP.

Objective

■ Configure the ISP router with DHCP, which will allow the Linksys router to pull an address from the pool you create. The Linksys router will then perform PAT on attached devices without having to be configured. Before you begin, reset the Linksys router to factory defaults by pressing the small button on the back of the router for 1 minute using a small pointy object, such as a pencil or paper clip.

Step 1. Cable and configure the equipment based on the topology in Figure 1-13.

Step 2. Configure the router with DHCP. Omit the router's IP address from the pool.

Step 3. The switch does not to be configured but should be cleaned of any previous configurations, especially VLAN information. Use the following commands to clear configurations:

```
Switch#delete flash:vlan.dat
Switch#erase startup-config or write erase
Switch#reload
```

Step 4. Connect to the Linksys router.

a. Open your web browser.

b. Enter **192.168.1.1** in the address bar. This is the default IP address of the Linksys router (see Figure 1-14).

Figure 1-14   Default Linksys IP Address

c. The router prompts you for a password (see Figure 1-15).

Figure 1-15   Linksys Password Prompt

d. Leave the username blank and enter the default password, admin (see Figure 1-16).

Figure 1-16   Linksys Administrator Login

e. The information shown in Figure 1-17 appears on the Linksys setup page.

Figure 1-17   Linksys Setup Page

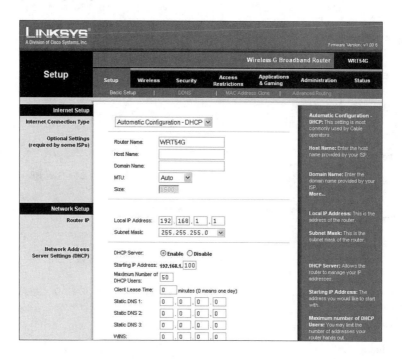

f. Under Network Setup, the default address of the Linksys router appears. With this option, you can use any address you choose, including those not included in RFC 1918.

Why is the router's IP address 192.168.1.1 rather than an address from the pool that has been created?

_____

What is the range of DHCP addresses used by the Linksys router?

_____

Step 5.   Open the command prompt dialog box and display the IP address of Host A and Host B (see Figure 1-18).

Figure 1-18   Displaying Host A and B IP Addresses

Step 6.   On the ISP router, enter the following command:

```
ISP#debug ip icmp
```

Step 7.   From Host A, ping the ISP router's Fast Ethernet interface.

The following information was displayed on the ISP router:

```
Router#

*Apr 14 07:51:53.955:   ICMP:   echo reply sent, src 200.100.28.1, dst
200.100.28.3

*Apr 14 07:51:54.953:   ICMP:   echo reply sent, src 200.100.28.1, dst
200.100.28.3

Router#

*Apr 14 07:51:55.955:   ICMP:   echo reply sent, src 200.100.28.1, dst
200.100.28.3

*Apr 14 07:51:56.956:   ICMP:   echo reply sent, src 200.100.28.1, dst
200.100.28.3

Router#

*Apr 14 07:52:06.760:   ICMP:   echo reply sent, src 200.100.28.1, dst
200.100.28.3

*Apr 14 07:52:07.750:   ICMP:   echo reply sent, src 200.100.28.1, dst
200.100.28.3

Router#

*Apr 14 07:52:08.752:   ICMP:   echo reply sent, src 200.100.28.1, dst
200.100.28.3

*Apr 14 07:52:09.753:   ICMP:   echo reply sent, src 200.100.28.1, dst
200.100.28.3

Router#
```

Why is the reply sent to the 200.100.28.3 address rather than the 192.168.100.2 address?

_____

_____

_____

Step 8.   Ping the 200.100.28.1 address from both hosts.

Why is only one address listed as the source instead of the IP address from each host?

_____

_____

CHAPTER 2

WAN Technologies

The Study Guide portion of this chapter uses a combination of matching, fill-in-the-blank, multiple-choice, and open-ended question exercises to test your knowledge of the theory of WAN devices, technologies, and connections such as Frame Relay, Integrated Services Digital Network (ISDN), digital subscriber line (DSL), and cable. This chapter also discusses WAN design and implementation.

This chapter contains no lab exercises.

Study Guide

WAN Technologies Overview

A WAN is a network that connects multiple LANs regardless of their physical location. A typical WAN uses several fundamental devices, such as routers, modems, WAN switches, channel service units/data service units (CSUs/DSUs), and communication servers. WANs use all seven layers of the OSI model but are generally focused within Layers 1 and 2. Layer 1 defines the type of connections used, along with their functionality. Layer 2 is where the encapsulation of data takes place, using protocols such as High-Level Data Link Control (HDLC) and Point-to-Point Protocol (PPP) to name just a few. WANs connect multiple locations (LANs) and use packet-switched technology to create virtual circuits between locations to make them look as though they are directly connected to one another.

Concept Questions

1. Explain the difference between LANs and WANs.

    _____

    _____

    _____

    _____

    _____

    _____

    _____

    _____

    _____

2. Compare and contrast the devices found on a LAN and those found on a WAN.

    _____

    _____

    _____

    _____

3. A company has multiple locations, and each location's router is from a different vendor. Would there be connectivity if each router is configured with HDLC? Why or why not?

    _____

    _____

4. Compare and contrast a switched virtual circuit (SVC) and a permanent virtual circuit (PVC).

    _____

    _____

    _____

    _____

    _____

5. Dialup connectivity is considered too slow, with low throughput speeds. It is generally being replaced by cable and DSL services. If this is the case, why is dialup still being used and still the most available connection available?

    _____

    _____

    _____

WAN Technologies

A network administrator may choose from several options when creating the physical links within a WAN. These options include analog dialup, ISDN, cable, DSL, Frame Relay, ATM, leased lines, and X.25. Analog dialup is what we know as regular dialup or 56k; this uses ordinary telephone lines to transmit data using analog signals rather than digital. ISDN usually carries two different channels:

- The B (bearer) channel, which carries voice and data

- The D (delta) channel, which is used for call setup and termination

There are two different types of ISDN:

- **Basic Rate Interface (BRI)**—Two 64-kbps B channels and one 16-kbps D channel

- **Primary Rate Interface (PRI)**—Twenty-three 64-kbps B channels and one 64-kbps D channel (equal in bandwidth to that of a T1)

Leased lines are connections to the provider network/ISP that a business must pay for monthly and can range from a 56-kbps line to an OC-48 line. In Frame Relay, there is no error checking, and Frame Relay uses PVCs and SVCs to provide connectivity between two locations. Asynchronous Transfer Mode (ATM) is a technology that provides low latency and low levels of jitter at high bandwidths by using cell technology; that is, data is split up into 53-byte cells to transmit faster. DSL, a dedicated user line, uses telephone lines to transmit data over high speeds by transmitting at higher frequencies than a regular phone line. Cable provides an always-on connection through coaxial cable, and users are in a shared environment.

Matching Terms

Match the definition on the left with the correct term on the right. Use each definition only one time.

Definitions

a. A full-time shared connection

b. An "always-on" connection that uses coaxial cable to carry signals to a modem

c. A path that is up during the duration of the connection that requires call setup and call termination

d. A pre-established dedicated connection available in different bandwidth options

e. A temporary permanent circuit dedicated from source to destination

f. A cell-switched technology that uses fixed cells at 53 bytes

g. A packet-switched technology that uses virtual circuits to connect multiple locations

h. Offers home and mobile users an inexpensive option for connecting to the Internet

i. A dedicated line from the source to the ISP that provides Internet access

j. Digital telephony and data transport services offered by regional telephone carriers

Terms

_____ ISDN BRI

_____ Analog dialup

_____ ATM

_____ PVC

_____ Frame Relay

_____ circuit-switched

_____ DSL

_____ leased line

_____ cable

_____ packet-switched

WAN Design

There are many different considerations when designing a WAN, such as the connections, LAN locations, how to connect them, and so on. Topology is also vital; primarily, star, full-mesh, and partial-mesh topologies are set up for WANs. Whether the WAN will use ATM, Frame Relay, or X.25 depends on the type of traffic that the WAN must handle. A hierarchy also proves useful to make the WAN more manageable, easier to troubleshoot, and scalable. Typically, the three-layer hierarchy used in WAN design consists of the access, distribution, and core layers. Security—protecting servers, LANs within the WAN, and so on—is also a primary concern when designing a WAN.

Concept Questions

1. You have a company that has four remote sites and a home office user (see Figure 2-1). Remote sites A, B, and C require permanent connections. Site D does not require a fixed connection but makes large file transfers once a day. The home office user needs access to resources located at headquarters and must be connected at all times. What type of WAN connection and speed should you use at headquarters? The remote sites? The home office?

Figure 2-1   WAN Connection Requirements

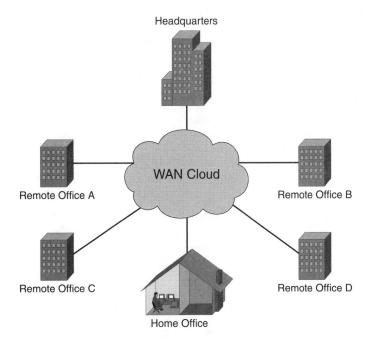

_____

_____

_____

_____

_____

2. What type of connection is best for a home office, and why?

_____

_____

_____

3. What types of DSL services are available to the consumer? Explain the differences between them.

_____

_____

_____

_____

_____

Lab Exercises

This chapter contains no lab exercises.

CHAPTER 3

PPP

The Study Guide portion of this chapter uses a combination of matching, fill-in-the-blank, multiple-choice, and open-ended question exercises to test your knowledge of the theory of serial point-to-point links, Point-to-Point Protocol (PPP), and authentication using Password Authentication Protocol (PAP) and Challenge Handshake Authentication Protocol (CHAP).

The Lab Exercises portion of this chapter includes all the online curriculum labs, a comprehensive lab, and a challenge lab to ensure that you have mastered the practical, hands-on skills needed for PPP and authentication configurations.

Study Guide

Serial Point-to-Point Links

The fundamentals of WAN technologies and communications are the links within a WAN. One of the more popular methods of transmission over a serial link is time-division multiplexing (TDM). Because serial links can transmit only 1 bit at a time over the link, TDM provides an organization data transmission through the use of timeslots. TDM prioritizes what data needs to be sent over the link and puts data into different categories, such as video, voice, and data. With TDM, multiple devices can transmit over one line. TDM acts as a train does—each timeslot contains one of the three categories of data, and they are just sent. However, the disadvantage of this is that if a device does not have any information to send, the empty timeslot remains part of the train being transmitted across the line.

Another aspect of WANs are demarcation points. These are the exchange of how responsibility from the provider to the customer and vice versa takes place. They may also separate the data circuit-terminating equipment (DCE) and data terminal equipment (DTE). The DCE is the device that provides the service, such as a connection to the Internet or to the WAN. The DTE, in most cases, is the customer using the service.

The DCE sets the rate at which the link operates (synchronously). Just like Ethernet, encapsulation is required for the data to be sent. HDLC is one form of encapsulation and is vendor-specific. All vendors (such as Cisco, 3Com, and so on) have their own version of High-Level Data Link Control (HDLC) that cannot communicate with another vendor's version. Typically, HDLC does not support multiple-link access protocols, but the Cisco version of HDLC has a Type field in the encapsulation that allows more than one protocol to operate on the same serial line. All versions of HDLC also add a flag at the beginning and the end of the datagram; the sole function of the flag is to say where the datagram begins and ends. To configure HDLC on a serial link, you must configure both connected serial interfaces on the router with the command **encapsulation hdlc**.

Concept Questions

1. You have a large network that has various connections to the Internet and that uses multiple Layer 3 protocols on the network. Security is a concern, and authentication is a must for remote users connecting to the network. The routers on the edge of the network are all Cisco, but those on the inside come from different vendors. The WAN encapsulation that you decide to use is PPP. Explain why this is the correct choice over HDLC.

    _____

    _____

    _____

    _____

    _____

2. The clock rate is normally set on the DCE end of a serial connection. Explain the purpose of the **clock rate** command and why the interface remains down if not set.

    _____

    _____

    _____

3. Explain the benefit of using TDM.

_____

_____

_____

PPP Authentication

PPP is another form of WAN encapsulation and is much different from HDLC. For one, it is an open-standard protocol that works in a multivendor environment. PPP provides the option of operating on asynchronous, synchronous, high-speed serial interfaces and ISDN. In addition, PPP allows authentication (optional configuration parameter) to be set to provide more security for a link. When establishing a link, PPP sends out a link control protocol (LCP) to negotiate the link's parameters before data transmission. After both routers negotiate the maximum transmission unit (MTU) and bandwidth over the link, authentication, if configured, takes place. The network control protocol (NCP) then chooses a network layer protocol to use, such as IP.

PPP may use two types of authentication:

- **Password Authentication Protocol (PAP)**—Uses a two-way handshake that asks the devices to authenticate only one time. It provides a simple security measure to verify the identity of the devices in question using a username and password. However, PAP is susceptible to hackers because it passes the username and password across the link in plain text, making it easier for the hacker to gain access.

- **Challenge Handshake Authentication Protocol (CHAP)**—Uses a three-way handshake and randomly authenticates the connecting device. CHAP is more secure than PAP because it is not susceptible to playback and because the challenges are encrypted using MD5 and are verified using a hash.

Concept Questions

1. Explain some of the functions of the LCP as it negotiates parameters of a link.

_____

_____

_____

_____

2. CHAP authentication is more secure than PAP because it uses MD5, a one-way hash to encode the password as it is sent across the link. Explain how a one-way hash works.

_____

_____

_____

_____

3. Explain the PPP session establishment phase.

_____

_____

_____

_____

_____

_____

_____

Configuring PPP

Encapsulation works on the border routers (ones that connect to the WAN). It does not matter what type of routers are on the inside of your network, because encapsulation has no bearing on them. To configure PPP on a serial interface, you must enter the command **encapsulation ppp**. To add the authentication, use the command **ppp authentication** followed by either **pap** or **chap**. To verify that the authentication has been configured properly on the interface, use the command **show interfaces serial** or **show interface serial** x or **show interface serial** x/y, where x or x/y is the number of the interface. If there is any problem with the configuration, debugging is a useful method of troubleshooting:

```
debug ppp [authentication | negotiation | packet | error | chap]
```

Concept Questions

1. Explain the purpose of the **ppp multilink** command and what would happen if it were not configured on an interface.

_____

_____

_____

2. Explain the difference between Stacker and Predictor compression mechanisms used by PPP.

_____

_____

_____

3. What information appears when you use the **debug ppp negotiation** command?

_____

_____

_____

_____

_____

_____

Chapter Review Questions

1. Which of the following are true of PAP? (Select two)

   A. It is a strong authentication protocol.

   B. It sends usernames and passwords across the link in plain text.

   C. It is a weak authentication protocol.

   D. It uses a one-way hash function.

2. Which of the following compression mechanisms is CPU-intensive?

   A. PAP

   B. Stacker

   C. Predictor

   D. CHAP

3. Which command enables PPP on an interface?

   A. Router(config)#**ppp encapsulation**

   B. Router(config)#**encapsulation ppp**

   C. Router(config-if)#**ppp encapsulation**

   D. Router(config-if)#**encapsulation ppp**

4. PPP can be configured on which of the following interface types? (Select all that apply)

   A. Serial interfaces

   B. Auxiliary interfaces

   C. Virtual interfaces

   D. High-speed serial interfaces

   E. ISDN BRI interfaces

   F. Loopback interfaces

5. What type of cable is used when connecting two DTE devices?

   A. RS-232

   B. Smart serial cable

   C. Null-modem

   D. V.35

6. Which of the following functions does the LCP perform? (Select all that apply)

   A. Detect misconfiguration errors

   B. Terminate a link

   C. Configure network layer protocols

   D. Determine whether a link is functioning

   E. Perform encryption

7. Which command provides load balancing across a PPP-configured interface?

   A. Callback

   B. Playback

   C. Overload

   D. Multilink

8. Which of the following are true of CHAP? (Select two)

    A. It uses a one-way hash.

    B. It uses a two-way hash.

    C. It uses a one-way handshake.

    D. It uses a two-way handshake.

    E. It uses a three-way handshake.

9. What is the location in the network called where responsibility between the telco and customer changes hands?

    A. Demarcation

    B. Local loop

    C. CSU/DSU

    D. DTE

    E. DCE

10. Which command displays real-time events as they happen on a PPP-configured interface? (Select all that apply)

    A. **show ppp interfaces**

    B. **show ppp authentication**

    C. **show ppp negotiation**

    D. **debug ppp interfaces**

    E. **debug ppp authentication**

    F. **debug ppp negotiation**

11. Which of the following features uses a magic number to detect loops?

    A. Authentication

    B. Negotiation

    C. Multilink

    D. Error detection

    E. Split horizon

12. Which of the following are true of PPP? (Select all that apply)

    A. Allows multiple network layer protocols to operate on the same link.

    B. Provides a separate NCP for every network layer protocol.

    C. Provides a separate LCP for every data link layer protocol.

    D. Does not support multiple network layer protocols across the same link.

    E. Each network layer protocol requires a separate LCP.

13. How should the username and passwords on each router be configured for PPP authentication? (Select two)

    A. Name of the person connecting to the device.

    B. Hostname of the local router.

    C. Hostname of the remote router.

    D. Same on both routers.

    E. Passwords can differ.

    F. Passwords must be the same.

14. What would happen if both PAP and CHAP were enabled on a router? (Select two)

    A. Negotiation would fail.

    B. The first method would be used during link negotiation.

    C. The peer could refuse to use the first method and try the second one instead.

    D. Authentication would fail if the peer router is configured for only one method only.

15. When does PAP authentication occur?

    A. After NCP establishes the link

    B. During the three-way handshake

    C. Only upon initial link establishment

    D. Periodically

16. Which of the following are true of PAP and CHAP authentication? (Select all that apply)

    A. It ensures that the caller has permission to establish a connection.

    B. It is an optional parameter.

    C. It reduces the amount of congestion on a link.

    D. Peer routers exchange authentication messages.

    E. It detects loops that may occur across the link.

17. What is the default encapsulation on Cisco serial interfaces?

    A. PPP

    B. ARAP

    C. IP

    D. IPX

    E. HDLC

18. Which command displays the state of interface channels and the type of cable connected?

    A. **show interface s0/0**

    B. **show ip interface s0/0**

    C. **show ip interface brief**

    D. **show controller s0/0**

    E. **show interfaces serial**

19. Which network layer protocols does NCP support? (Select two)

    A. IPCP

    B. IPNP

    C. ICMP

    D. IPXCP

    E. IPXNP

20. Which of the following are not protected against by PAP? (Select all that apply)

    A. Callback attacks

    B. Playback attacks

    C. Random challenges

    D. Trial-and-error attacks

Lab Exercises

Curriculum Lab 3-1: Troubleshooting a Serial Interface (3.1.7)

Figure 3-1   Topology for Lab 3-1

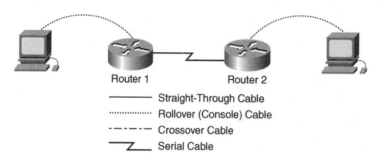

——————— Straight-Through Cable
·················· Rollover (Console) Cable
– – – – – Crossover Cable
——Z—— Serial Cable

Table 3-1   Lab Equipment Configuration

Router Designation	Router Name	Interface Type	Serial 0 Address
Router 1	London	DCE	192.168.15.1
Router 2	Paris	DTE	192.168.15.2

The enable secret password for both routers is **class**.

The enable, vty, and console password for both routers is **cisco**.

The subnet mask for both routers is 255.255.255.0.

Objectives

- Configure a serial interface on two routers.

- Use **show** commands to troubleshoot connectivity issues.

Background/Preparation

Cable a network that is similar to the one in Figure 3-1. You can use any router that meets the interface requirements in Figure 3-1 (that is, 800, 1600, 1700, 2500, and 2600 routers, or a combination). See the information in Appendix C, "Router Interface Summary Chart," to correctly specify the interface identifiers based on the equipment in your lab. The 1721 series routers produced the configuration output in this lab. Another router might produce slightly different output. Execute the following tasks on each router unless you are specifically instructed otherwise.

Start a HyperTerminal session.

Implement the procedure documented in Appendix E, "Erasing and Reloading the Router," on all routers before you continue with this lab.

Task 1: Configure the Routers

Configure the hostname, console, vty, and enable passwords according to Table 3-1. If you have difficulty doing this, see Lab 1-1, "Configuring NAT."

Task 2: Configure the Paris Interface

Configure the Paris router serial interface as follows:

```
Paris(config)#interface serial 0
Paris(config-if)#ip address 192.168.15.2 255.255.255.0
Paris(config-if)#clock rate 56000
Paris(config-if)#no shutdown
Paris(config-if)#exit
Paris(config)#exit
```

Task 3: Configure the London Interface

Configure the London router serial interface as follows:

```
London(config)#interface serial 0
London(config-if)#ip address 192.168.15.1 255.255.255.0
London(config-if)#no shutdown
London(config-if)#exit
London(config)#exit
```

Task 4: Save the Configuration

To save the configuration of the Paris and London router serial interfaces, enter the following:

```
London#copy running-config startup-config
```

```
Paris#copy running-config startup-config
```

Task 5: Enter the Command show interface serial 0 (See Appendix C) on London

```
London#show interface serial 0
```

This shows the details of interface serial 0.

Answer the following questions:

Serial 0 is ____, and line protocol is _____.

What type of problem is indicated in the last statement? _____

What is the Internet address? _____

What is the encapsulation type? _____

Task 6: Enter the Command show interface serial 0 (See Appendix C) on Paris

Paris#**show interface serial 0**

This shows the details of interface serial 0.

Answer the following questions:

Serial 0 is ____, and line protocol is _____.

What is the Internet address? _____

What is the encapsulation type? _____

To what OSI layer does "Encapsulation" refer? _____

Why is the interface down?

_____

Task 7: Correct the Clock Location

The **clock rate** statement has been placed on the wrong interface. It is currently placed on the Paris router, but the London router is the DCE. Remove the **clock rate** statement from the Paris router by using the **no** version of the command. Then, add it to the London router's configuration.

Task 8: Enter the Command show interface serial 0 on Paris

Paris#**show interface serial 0**

Serial 0 is ____, and line protocol is ____.

What is the difference in the Line and Protocol status that was recorded on Paris earlier? Why?

_____

Task 9: Verify That the Serial Connection Is Functioning by Pinging the Serial Interface of the Other Router

London#**ping** 192.168.15.2

Paris#**ping** 192.168.15.1

From London, can you ping the Paris router's serial interface? _____

From Paris, can you ping the London router's serial interface? _____

If the answer is no for either question, troubleshoot the router configurations to find the error. Then, do the pings again until the answer to both questions is yes.

After you complete the previous tasks, log off (by entering **exit**) and turn the router off. Then, remove and store the cables and adapter.

Curriculum Lab 3-2: Configuring PPP Encapsulation (3.3.2)

Figure 3-2   Topology for Lab 3-2

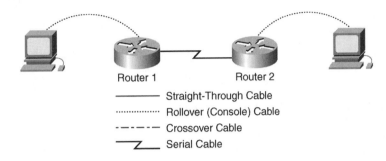

Router 1   Router 2

——————————— Straight-Through Cable

·························· Rollover (Console) Cable

– – – – – Crossover Cable

———Z——— Serial Cable

Table 3-2   Lab Equipment Configuration

Router Designation	Router Name	Interface Type	Serial 0 Address
Router 1	Washington	DCE	192.168.15.1
Router 2	Dublin	DTE	192.168.15.2

The enable secret password for both routers is **class**.

The enable, vty, and console password for both routers is **cisco**.

The subnet mask for both routers is 255.255.255.0.

Objectives

- Configure the serial interfaces on two routers with the PPP protocol.

- Test the link for connectivity.

Background/Preparation

Cable a network that is similar to the one in Figure 3-2. You can use any router that meets the interface requirements in Figure 3-2 (that is, 800, 1600, 1700, 2500, and 2600 routers, or a combination). See the information in Appendix C to correctly specify the interface identifiers based on the equipment in your lab. The 1721 series routers produced the configuration output in this lab. Another router might produce slightly different output. Execute the following tasks on each router unless you are specifically instructed otherwise.

Start a HyperTerminal session.

Implement the procedure documented in Appendix E on all routers before you continue with this lab.

Task 1: Configure the Routers

Configure the hostname, console, vty, and enable passwords according to Table 3-2. If you have difficulty doing this, see Lab 1-1, "Configuring NAT."

Task 2: Configure the Dublin Interface

Configure the Dublin router serial interface as follows:

```
Dublin(config)#interface serial 0
Dublin(config-if)#ip address 192.168.15.2 255.255.255.0
Dublin(config-if)#no shutdown
Dublin(config-if)#exit
Dublin(config)#exit
```

Task 3: Configure the Washington Interface

Configure the Washington router serial interface as follows:

```
Washington(config)#interface serial 0
Washington(config-if)#ip address 192.168.15.1 255.255.255.0
Washington(config-if)#clock rate 64000
Washington(config-if)#no shutdown
Washington(config-if)#exit
Washington(config)#exit
```

Task 4: Save the Configuration

To save the Dublin and Washing router serial interfaces, use the following commands:

```
Dublin#copy running-config startup-config


Washington#copy running-config startup-config
```

Task 5: Enter the Command show interface serial 0 (See Appendix C) on Washington

```
Washington#show interface serial 0
```

This shows the details of interface serial 0.

Serial 0 is _____, and line protocol is _____.

The Internet address is _____.

Encapsulation is _____.

Task 6: Enter the Command show interface serial 0 (See Appendix C) on Dublin

```
Dublin#show interface serial 0
```

This shows the details of interface serial 0.

Serial 0 is _____, and line protocol is _____.

The Internet address is _____.

Encapsulation is _____.

Task 7: Change the Encapsulation Type

Change the encapsulation type to PPP by entering **encapsulation ppp** at the interface serial 0 configuration mode prompt on both routers:

```
Washington(config-if)#encapsulation ppp
Dublin(config-if)#encapsulation ppp
```

Task 8: Enter the Command show interface serial 0 on Washington

```
Washington#show interface serial 0
```

What is the encapsulation type? _____

Task 9: Enter the Command show interface serial 0 on Dublin

```
Dublin#show interface serial 0
```

What is the encapsulation type? _____

Task 10: Verify That the Serial Connection Is Functioning by Pinging the Serial Interface of the Other Router

```
Washington#ping 192.168.15.2
```

```
Dublin#ping 192.168.15.1
```

From Washington, can you ping the Dublin router's serial interface? _____

From Dublin, can you ping the Washington router's serial interface? _____

If the answer is no for either question, troubleshoot the router configurations to find the error. Then, do the pings again until the answer to both questions is yes.

_____

_____

_____

_____

_____

_____

_____

_____

_____

_____

_____

After you complete the previous tasks, log off (by entering **exit**) and turn the router off. Then, remove and store the cables and adapter.

Curriculum Lab 3-3: Configuring PPP Authentication (3.3.3)

Figure 3-3 Topology for Lab 3-3

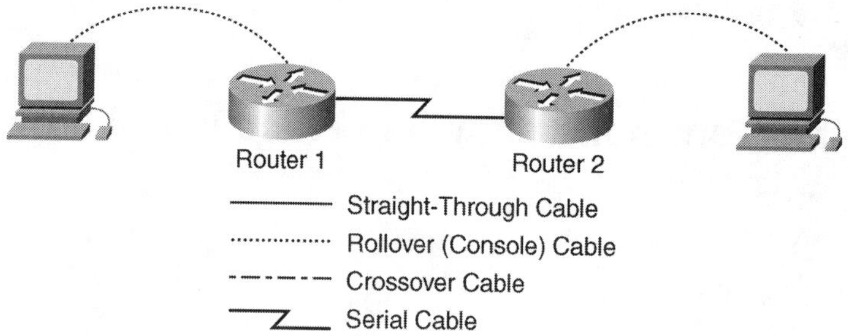
Router 1
Router 2
Straight-Through Cable
Rollover (Console) Cable
Crossover Cable
Serial Cable

Table 3-3 Lab Equipment Configuration

Router Designation	Router Name	Interface Type	Serial 0 Address
Router 1	Madrid	DCE	192.168.15.1
Router 2	Tokyo	DTE	192.168.15.2

The enable secret password for both routers is **class**.

The enable, vty, and console password for both routers is **cisco**.

The subnet mask for both routers is 255.255.255.0.

Objective

- Configure PPP authentication by using CHAP on two routers.

Background/Preparation

Cable a network that is similar to the one in Figure 3-3. You can use any router that meets the interface requirements in Figure 3-3 (that is, 800, 1600, 1700, 2500, and 2600 routers, or a combination). See the information in Appendix C to correctly specify the interface identifiers based on the equipment in your lab. The 1721 series routers produced the configuration output in this lab. Another router might produce slightly different output. Execute the following tasks on each router unless you are specifically instructed otherwise.

Start a HyperTerminal session.

Implement the procedure documented in Appendix E on all routers before you continue with this lab.

Task 1: Configure the Routers

Configure the hostname, console, vty, and enable passwords according to Table 3-3. If you have difficulty doing this, see Lab 1-1, "Configuring NAT."

Task 2: Configure the Tokyo Interface

Configure the Tokyo router serial interface as follows:

```
Tokyo(config)#interface serial 0
Tokyo(config-if)#ip address 192.168.15.2 255.255.255.0
Tokyo(config-if)#encapsulation ppp
Tokyo(config-if)#no shutdown
Tokyo(config-if)#exit
Tokyo(config)#exit
```

Task 3: Configure the Madrid Interface

Configure the Madrid router serial interface as follows:

```
Madrid(config)#interface serial 0
Madrid(config-if)#ip address 192.168.15.1 255.255.255.0
Madrid(config-if)#clock rate 64000
Madrid(config-if)#encapsulation ppp
Madrid(config-if)#no shutdown
Madrid(config-if)#exit
Madrid(config)#exit
```

Task 4: Save the Configuration

To save the Tokyo and Madrid serial interface configurations, use the following commands:

```
Tokyo#copy running-config startup-config
Madrid#copy running-config startup-config
```

Task 5: Enter the Command show interface serial 0 on Madrid

```
Madrid#show interface serial 0
```

What is the encapsulation type? _____

Task 6: Enter the Command show interface serial 0 on Tokyo

```
Tokyo#show interface serial 0
```

What is the encapsulation type? _____

Task 7: Verify That the Serial Connection Is Functioning by Pinging the Serial Interface of the Other Router

```
Madrid#ping 192.168.15.2
```

```
Tokyo#ping 192.168.15.1
```

If the pings are unsuccessful, troubleshoot the router configurations to find the error. Then, do the pings again until both pings succeed.

Task 8: Configure PPP Authentication

Configure usernames and passwords on the Madrid router. The passwords must be the same on both routers. The username must reflect the other router's hostname exactly. (It is case-sensitive.)

```
Madrid(config)#username Tokyo password cisco
Madrid(config)#interface serial 0
Madrid(config-if)#ppp authentication chap
```

Task 9: Verify That the Serial Connection Is Functioning

Verify that the serial connection is functioning by pinging the serial interface of the other router:

```
Madrid#ping 192.168.15.2
```

Did the ping succeed? _____

Why? _____

Task 10: Configure PPP Authentication

Configure usernames and passwords on the Tokyo router. The passwords must be the same on both routers. The usernames must reflect the other router's hostname exactly (they are case-sensitive).

```
Tokyo(config)#username Madrid password cisco
Tokyo(config)#interface serial 0
Tokyo(config-if)#ppp authentication chap
```

Task 11: Verify That the Serial Connection Is Functioning

Verify that the serial connection is functioning by pinging the serial interface of the other router:

```
Tokyo#ping 192.168.15.1
```

Did the ping succeed? _____

Why? _____

After you complete the previous tasks, log off (by entering **exit**) and turn the router off. Then, remove and store the cables and adapter.

Curriculum Lab 3-4: Verifying PPP Configuration (3.3.4)

Figure 3-4   Topology for Lab 3-4

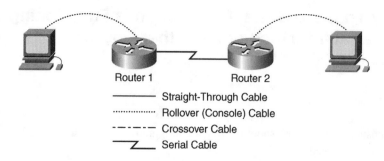

Router 1   Router 2

——————   Straight-Through Cable

·············   Rollover (Console) Cable

– – – – –   Crossover Cable

—–Z–—   Serial Cable

Table 3-4   Lab Equipment Configuration

Router Designation	Router Name	Interface Type	Serial 0 Address
Router 1	Brasilia	DCE	192.168.15.1
Router 2	Warsaw	DTE	192.168.15.2

The enable secret password for both routers is **class**.

The enable, vty, and console password for both routers is **cisco**.

The subnet mask for both routers is 255.255.255.0.

Objectives

- Configure a serial interface on two routers with the PPP protocol.

- Verify and test the link for connectivity.

Background/Preparation

Cable a network that is similar to the one in Figure 3-4. You can use any router that meets the interface requirements in Figure 3-4 (that is, 800, 1600, 1700, 2500, and 2600 routers, or a combination). See the information in Appendix C to correctly specify the interface identifiers based on the equipment in your lab. The 1721 series routers produced the configuration output in this lab. Another router might produce slightly different output. Execute the following tasks on each router unless you are specifically instructed otherwise.

Start a HyperTerminal session.

Implement the procedure documented in Appendix E on all routers before you continue with this lab.

Task 1: Configure the Routers

Configure the hostname, console, vty, and enable passwords according to Table 3-4. If you have difficulty doing this, see Lab 1-1, "Configuring NAT."

Task 2: Configure the Warsaw

Configure the Warsaw router serial interface as follows:

```
Warsaw(config)#interface serial 0
Warsaw(config-if)#ip address 192.168.15.2 255.255.255.0
Warsaw(config-if)#no shutdown
Warsaw(config-if)#exit
Warsaw(config)#exit
```

Task 3: Configure the Brasilia Interface

Configure the Brasilia router serial interface as follows:

```
Brasilia(config)#interface serial 0
Brasilia(config-if)#ip address 192.168.15.1 255.255.255.0
Brasilia(config-if)#clock rate 64000
Brasilia(config-if)#no shutdown
Brasilia(config-if)#exit
Brasilia(config)#exit
```

Task 4: Save the Configuration

To save the Warsaw and Brasilia router serial interface configurations, use the following commands:

```
Warsaw#copy running-config startup-config
```

```
Brasilia#copy running-config startup-config
```

Task 5: Enter the Command show interface serial 0 (See Appendix C) on Brasilia

```
Brasilia#show interface serial 0
```

This shows the details of interface serial 0.

The encapsulation type is _____.

Task 6: Enter the Command show interface serial 0 (See Appendix C) on Warsaw

```
Warsaw#show interface serial 0
```

This shows the details of interface serial 0.

The encapsulation type is _____.

Task 7: Turn on PPP Debugging

Turn on the PPP debug function on both routers by entering **debug ppp event** at the privileged EXEC mode prompt. Note: For the 2600 router, use the command **debug ppp tasks**.

Task 8: Change the Encapsulation Type

Step 1.   Change the encapsulation type to PPP by entering **encapsulation ppp** at the interface serial 0 configuration mode prompt on both routers:

```
Brasilia(config-if)#encapsulation ppp
```

```
Warsaw(config-if)#encapsulation ppp
```

What did the debug function report when the PPP encapsulation was applied to each router?

_____

_____

_____

_____

_____

_____

Step 2.   Turn off the debug function by entering **undebug all** at the privileged EXEC mode prompt.

Task 9: Enter the Command show interface serial 0 on Brasilia

Brasilia#**show interface serial 0**

The encapsulation type is _____.

Task 10: Enter the Command show interface serial 0 on Warsaw

Warsaw#**show interface serial 0**

The encapsulation type is _____.

Task 11: Verify That the Serial Connection Is Functioning

Step 1.   Ping the other router to verify that there is connectivity between the two routers.

Brasilia#**ping 192.168.15.2**

Warsaw#**ping 192.168.15.1**

From Brasilia, can you ping the Warsaw router's serial interface? _____

From Warsaw, can you ping the Brasilia router's serial interface? _____

Step 2.   If the answer is no for either question, troubleshoot the router configurations to find the error. Then, do the pings again until the answer to both questions is yes.

Step 3.   After you complete the previous tasks, log off (by entering **exit**) and turn the router off. Then, remove and store the cables and adapter.

Curriculum Lab 3-5: Troubleshooting PPP Configuration (3.3.5)

Figure 3-5   Topology for Lab 3-5

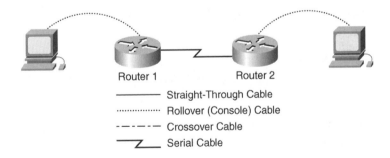

Table 3-5   Lab Equipment Configuration

Router Designation	Router Name	Interface Type	Serial 0 Address
Router 1	London	DCE	192.168.15.1
Router 2	Paris	DTE	192.168.15.2

The enable secret password for both routers is **class**.

The enable, vty, and console password for both routers is **cisco**.

The subnet mask for both routers is 255.255.255.0.

Objectives

- Configure a PPP on the serial interfaces of two routers.

- Use **show** and **debug** commands to troubleshoot connectivity issues.

Background/Preparation

Cable a network that is similar to the one in Figure 3-5. You can use any router that meets the interface requirements in Figure 3-5 (that is, 800, 1600, 1700, 2500, and 2600 routers, or a combination). See the information in Appendix C to correctly specify the interface identifiers based on the equipment in your lab. The 1721 series routers produced the configuration output in this lab. Another router might produce slightly different output. Execute the following tasks on each router unless you are specifically instructed otherwise.

Start a HyperTerminal session.

Implement the procedure documented in Appendix E on all routers before you continue with this lab.

Task 1: Configure the Routers

Configure the hostname, console, vty, and enable passwords according to Table 3-5. If you have difficulty doing this, see Lab 1-1, "Configuring NAT."

Task 2: Configure the Paris Interface

Configure the Paris router serial interface as follows:

```
Paris(config)#interface serial 0
Paris(config-if)#ip address 192.168.15.2 255.255.255.0
Paris(config-if)#clock rate 56000
Paris(config-if)#no shutdown
Paris(config-if)#exit
Paris(config)#exit
```

Task 3: Configure the London Interface

Configure the London router serial interface as follows:

```
London(config)#interface serial 0
London(config-if)#ip address 192.168.15.1 255.255.255.0
London(config-if)#encapsulation ppp
London(config-if)#no shutdown
London(config-if)#exit
London(config)#exit
```

Task 4: Save the Configuration

To save the Paris and London router serial interface configurations, use the following commands:

```
Paris#copy running-config startup-config
London#copy running-config startup-config
```

Task 5: Enter the Command show interface serial 0 (See Appendix C) on London

London#**show interface serial 0**

This shows the details of interface serial 0.

List the following information discovered from issuing this command:

- Serial 0 is _____, and line protocol is _____.

- What type of problem is indicated in the last statement? _____

- The Internet address is _____.

- The encapsulation type is _____.

Task 6: Enter the Command show interface serial 0 (See Appendix C) on Paris

Paris#**show interface serial 0**

This shows the details of interface serial 0.

List the following information discovered from issuing this command:

- Serial 0 is _____, and line protocol is _____.

- The Internet address is _____.

- The encapsulation type is _____.

- To what OSI layer does "Encapsulation" refer? _____

If the serial interface were configured, why did the **show interface serial 0** output show that the interface is down?

_____

Task 7: Correct the Clock Location

The **clock rate** statement has been placed on the wrong interface. It is currently placed on the Paris router, but the London router is the DCE. Remove the **clock rate** statement from the Paris router by using the **no** version of the command, and then add it to the configuration for the London router.

_____

_____

_____

_____

Task 8: Enter the Command show cdp neighbors on London

Is there output from the command? _____

Should there be output? _____

Task 9: Enter the Command debug ppp negotiation on London

It might take 60 seconds or more before output occurs.

Is there output? _____

What is the output saying? _____

Is there a problem with PPP encapsulation on the London router or the Paris router? _____

Why? _____

What encapsulations were listed for the interfaces?

London? _____

Paris? _____

Is there an issue with the preceding answers? _____

What is the issue? _____

Task 10: Enter the command debug ppp negotiation on Paris

Enter the command **debug ppp negotiation** on the Paris router at the privileged EXEC mode prompt.

Is there output from the **debug** command? _____

Task 11: Correct the Encapsulation Type

Convert the encapsulation to PPP on the Paris router.

Is there output from the **debug** command? _____

Does it confirm link establishment? _____

Task 12: Enter the command show interface serial 0 on Paris

`Paris#`**`show interface serial 0`**

Serial0 is _____, and line protocol is _____.

The encapsulation type is _____.

What is the difference between the Line and Protocol status recorded on Paris earlier? Why?

Task 13: Verify That the Serial Connection Is Functioning by Pinging the Serial Interface of the Other Router

`London#`**`ping 192.168.15.1`**

`Paris#`**`ping 192.168.15.2`**

From London, can you ping the serial interface on the Paris router? _____

From Paris, can you ping the serial interface on the London router? _____

If the answer is no for either question, troubleshoot the router configurations to find the error. Then, do the pings again until the answer to both questions is yes.

After you complete the previous tasks, log off (by entering **exit**) and turn the router off. Then, remove and store the cables and adapter.

Challenge Lab 3-6: Configuring PPP with NAT, DHCP, and VLANs

You are a newly hired network administrator for a start-up company (ACME) that wants to you to create a secure connection to an ISP. You are also responsible for IP addressing, VLAN assignment, DHCP, and NAT. Figure 3-6 shows the network topology for this lab.

Figure 3-6   Network Topology for Lab 3-6

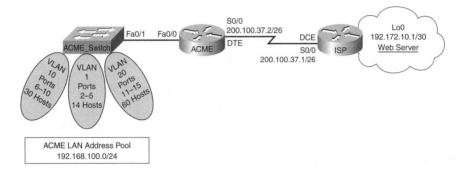

Objectives

■ Configure PPP with authentication.

■ Configure DHCP, NAT, and PAT.

■ Configure the ISP as a web server and verify connectivity via a web browser from hosts on the ACME LAN.

Task 1

Step 1.   Cable the equipment.

Step 2.   Protect the privileged mode using an encrypted password of **class**.

Step 3.   Ensure that the command output is not interrupted by router output.

Step 4.   Restrict remote access to devices using **cisco** as the password.

Task 2

Step 1.   Based on the diagram in Figure 3-6, create an addressing scheme to accommodate users on the ACME LAN.

Step 2.   Create three VLANs on ACME_Switch:

■ VLAN 1: default name

■ VLAN 10: Marketing VLAN

■ VLAN 20: HR_Dept

Step 3.   Assign VLANs to the appropriate interfaces based on the diagram in Figure 3-6.

Step 4.   Configure inter-VLAN routing on the ACME router.

Task 3

Step 1.   Configure the ACME router as a DHCP server.

Step 2.   Create a separate DHCP pool for each subnet.

Step 3.   Exclude the first three addresses from each DHCP pool.

Step 4.   Verify that the workstations obtain the correct information from the server.

Task 4

Step 1.   Use the spare addresses from the WAN link to create your NAT pools.

Step 2.   Configure dynamic NAT for VLAN 1 and the Marketing VLAN.

Step 3.   Use one global address for HR_Dept to access the outside world.

Task 5

Configure both routers to use PPP as the encapsulation protocol.

_____

_____

_____

_____

_____

_____

Task 6

Configure a secure authentication on both routers that protects against callback.

_____

_____

_____

_____

_____

_____

_____

_____

Task 7

Verify the configuration using the appropriate commands. Do not limit yourself to using only the **show running-config** command. The lab is accomplished when all hosts can access the web server via the web browser.

CHAPTER 4

ISDN and DDR

The Study Guide portion of this chapter uses a combination of multiple-choice and open-ended question exercises to test your knowledge of the theory of ISDN standards, concepts, and reference points.

The Lab Exercises portion of this chapter includes all the online curriculum labs and a challenge lab to ensure that you have mastered the practical, hands-on skills needed for dialer interfaces, dialer maps, and dialer profiles.

Study Guide

ISDN Concepts

ISDN is a WAN technology that serves as a solution for offices using digitized phone lines. ISDN allows for faster call setup and transfer of data, video, and audio than traditional analog dialup. Call setup and termination are done on a separate channel (D or delta channel), which is called *out-of-band signaling*. Data is transmitted over a separate channel called the B or bearer channel. Each B channel provides 64 kbps of bandwidth, whereas the D channel has 16 kbps of bandwidth (ISDN Basic Rate Interface [BRI]) or 64 kbps (ISDN Primary Rate Interface [PRI]). ISDN PRI in North America consists of 23 B channels and one D channel. It is an inexpensive, cost-effective alternative to a dedicated T1 connection. The European equivalent to an ISDN PRI is called an E. It consists of 30 B channels and a single D channel.

ISDN has three sets of standards:

- The E protocols, which define the telephone network standards
- The I protocols, which relate to ISDN concepts and terms
- The Q protocols, which determine the operation of signaling and switching

During the call setup process, the phone number is transmitted to the local ISDN switch via the D channel. It is then forwarded to another ISDN switch using the Signaling System 7 (SS7) signaling protocol. The number is passed to the destination, which sends its acknowledgment back through the ISDN switches to the caller; from here, the connection is officially established. Switch types that give a set of call setup needs must also be configured depending on which type the service provider is using. Service provider identifiers (SPIDs) are also provided by the Internet service provider (ISP) as a mandatory component to connect to the local ISDN switch. SPIDs are actually phone lines that are dialed to establish a connection.

Concept Questions

1. Compare ISDN BRI and PRI.

   _____

   _____

   _____

2. Explain the function of the ISDN delta and bearer channels.

   _____

   _____

   _____

3. Explain the difference between in-band and out-of-band signaling.

   _____

   _____

   _____

   _____

   _____

ISDN Configuration

ISDN BRI must be configured with the switch type and SPIDs. The switch type can be configured in either global configuration mode or interface mode. You use global configuration mode when connecting to multiple switches that are of the same type. You use interface mode when connecting to multiple switches of different types. This requires the exact switch type to be configured on the appropriate interface. In global configuration mode, configure the switch type using the command **isdn switch-type** *switch-type*.

You can set up two SPIDs on ISDN BRI, one for each B channel. Go into the BRI interface and enter **isdn spid1** [*spid-number*] and **isdn spid2** [*spid-number*].

In ISDN PRI, you must also configure the switch type. Specify in global configuration mode where the T1/E1 card is located with the command **controller** [**t1** | **e1**] *slot/port*. This is similar to going into an interface.

When inside controller mode, set the framing with either **framing** [**sf** | **esf**] when configuring T1 lines or **framing** [**crc4** | **no-crc4**] for E1 lines. Also, inside controller mode, you must specify the signaling with the command **linecode** [**ami** | **b8zs** | **hdb3**]. To verify all configurations, use the commands **show isdn active**, **show dialer**, and **show interface bri** [*slot/port*].

Concept Questions

1. Explain the purpose of identifying the appropriate ISDN switch type.

   _____

   _____

   _____

   _____

2. Explain the function of a SPID.

   _____

   _____

   _____

3. What information appears when you enter the **show isdn active** command?

   _____

DDR Configuration

Dial-on-demand routing (DDR) is a method that allows the ISDN line to be triggered only when certain types of traffic, called interesting traffic, attempt to cross the line. This interesting traffic is filtered by a set of predetermined criteria set in a dialer list. When the line is turned on, all traffic can cross, even that considered "boring." After all interesting traffic has finished crossing the ISDN line, the line terminates until the next batch of interesting traffic passes through. To specify what the interesting traffic will be, use the **dialer-list** command. For example, to allow all IP traffic to be considered interesting, you use the command **dialer-list 1 protocol ip permit**. You must apply the dialer list to the interface with the command **dialer-group** [*list-number*].

Legacy DDR is a basic method of setting up dialer characteristics that must be applied to an interface. Setting up legacy DDR requires configuring static routes and dialer information and predetermining interesting traffic. The dialer information consists of the dialer map, encapsulation, authentication, and idle timeout. To configure the dialer map, use the command **dialer map** [*protocol*] [*next-hop-address*] **name** [*hostname*] [*dial-string*] while inside the interface. Use the **dialer idle-timeout** command on the interface to specify when the line will disconnect after all interesting traffic has been transmitted.

A more flexible alternative to dialer maps is dialer profiles. Instead of statically configuring dialer parameters onto an interface and changing them every time the call setup requirements change, dialer profiles are automatically assigned to the interface every time the call requirements change. Create a dialer profile with the command **interface dialer** [*number*], and assign the profile with the encapsulation, an IP address, and a dialer string using the command **dialer remote-name** [*name*]. Go into the physical ISDN interface and use the command **dialer pool-member** [*pool-number*] **priority** [*number*] to make the interface part of a dialer pool. If multiple calls are placed simultaneously, the pool with the highest priority dials out first. Verify all DDR configurations with the commands **show isdn status**, **show isdn active**, and **show dialer**.

Concept Questions

1. Why is it better to use static routes rather than dynamic routes across an ISDN connection?

    _____

    _____

2. Explain the function of a SPID within a dialer map.

    _____

    _____

3. Compare a dialer map to a dialer profile.

    _____

    _____

    _____

    _____

Chapter Review Questions

For multiple-choice questions 1 through 20, circle the correct answers. Some questions have more than one answer.

1. What are the benefits of ISDN? (Select three)

    A. Always-on connection

    B. Cost-effective

    C. Faster call setup and termination

    D. Fiber connection

    E. Can transport video, voice, and data simultaneously

2. What set of protocols deal with ISDN telephone network standards?

    A. I protocols

    B. Q protocols

    C. IEEE protocols

    D. E protocols

    E. HDLC-derived protocols

3. Which channel in ISDN is used for call setup and termination?

    A. B channel

    B. D channel

    C. C channel

    D. BRI channel

    E. PRI channel

4. In North America, ISDN PRI uses 23 bearer channels and one delta channel to equal the bandwidth of a T1. What does this make ISDN PRI most efficient for?

    A. A substitute for using a T1 line

    B. A fallback in case the original line malfunctions

    C. No efficiency whatsoever

    D. Primary always-on connection

5. Which device in an ISDN connection is responsible for converting the four-wire signal to a two-wire digitized ISDN signal?

    A. TA

    B. TE1

    C. NT2

    D. NT1

    E. TE2

6. What factors affect which switch type a private network will use on its ISDN router? (Select two)

    A. Switch type used by the carrier

    B. Protocols that are being run

    C. Country/region of the private network

    D. Whether the connection is BRI or PRI

    E. SPIDs being used

7. What modes on a router can a switch type be configured in? (Select two)

    A. Router>

    B. Router#

    C. Router(config)#

    D. Router(config-if)#

    E. Router(config-subif)#

8. On ISDN BRI, what is the maximum number of SPIDs you can configure per bearer channel?

    A. 1

    B. 2

    C. 3

    D. The SPID is configured for the BRI interface.

    E. None

9. What command enables you to make configurations when using ISDN PRI?

   A. Router(config)#**interface pri** *slot/port*

   B. Router(config)#**interface** *t1/e1 slot/port*

   C. Router(config)#**controller pri** *slot/port*

   D. Router(config)#**controller** *t1/e1 slot/port*

   E. Router(config)#**interface pri** *t1/e1*

10. What command shows the time remaining on an ISDN call?

   A. **show isdn status**

   B. **show isdn active**

   C. **show interface bri0/0**

   D. **debug isdn q921**

   E. **show running-configuration**

11. How do you configure DDR? (Select three)

   A. Determine interesting traffic with a dialer list.

   B. Set up static routes.

   C. Disable ISDN before setting up DDR.

   D. Set up dialer maps.

   E. DDR is on by default on Cisco routers.

12. When configuring dialer information, what are the requirements for setup? (Select three)

   A. Encapsulation

   B. Dialer maps

   C. Access lists

   D. Idle timeouts

   E. Static routes

13. What are some advantages of using dialer profiles over legacy DDR and dialer maps? (Select three)

   A. One ISDN interface can take on different characteristics based on the calls.

   B. You can configure each B channel on a different subnet.

   C. All aspects of dialer profiles are dynamic and do not have to be configured.

   D. Each B channel can have different DDR parameters.

   E. Dialer profiles have no advantages.

14. What command assigns an ISDN interface to a dialer pool?

   A. Router(config-if)#**dialer pool-member** *number*

   B. Router(config)#**interface bri** *slot/port* **dialer-pool member** *number*

   C. Router(config-if)#**ip assign dialer pool-member** *number*

   D. Router(config)#**dialer pool-member** *number*

   E. Router(config-if)#**pool-member dialer** *number*

15. Which command displays information about the BRI interface's three layers?

- **A. show isdn status**
- **B. show isdn active**
- **C. show interface bri0/0**
- **D. debug isdn q921**
- **E. debug isdn q931**

16. What command helps troubleshoot call setup and termination?

- **A. debug ppp error**
- **B. debug isdn q931**
- **C. debug ppp negotiation**
- **D. debug isdn q921**
- **E. debug ppp authentication**

17. What is the name of the reference point that connects the customer's switching device and enables calls between the various types of customer premises equipment?

- **A.** R
- **B.** S
- **C.** T
- **D.** U
- **E.** NT1
- **F.** NT2

18. A dialer profile consists of which three elements?

- **A.** Dialer interface
- **B.** Dialer pool
- **C.** Virtual interface
- **D.** Physical interface
- **E.** Static routes
- **F.** Dynamic routes

19. What does an ISDN PRI use for T1/E1 connections?

- **A.** ISDN switch
- **B.** DTE
- **C.** DCE
- **D.** CSU/DSU
- **E.** LMI extensions

20. Each TE1 must be manually or statically assigned a unique identifier. What range of numbers is used when statically assigning an identifier to a TE1 device?

- **A.** 0–63
- **B.** 1–63
- **C.** 64–126
- **D.** 64–128

Lab Exercises

Curriculum Lab 4-1: Configuring ISDN BRI (U-Interface) (4.2.1)

Figure 4-1   Topology for Lab 4-1

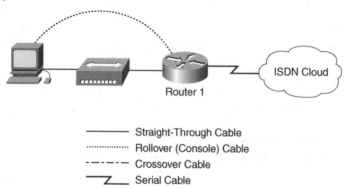

```
———————  Straight-Through Cable
··············  Rollover (Console) Cable
— — — — —  Crossover Cable
⌐Z___  Serial Cable
```

Table 4-1   Lab Equipment Configuration

Router Designation	Router Name	Fast Ethernet0 Address/Subnet Mask	BRI 0 Address	Adtran Connection
Router 1	Ottawa	192.168.14.1/24	—	BRI 1

The enable secret password for this router is **class**.

The enable, vty, and console password for this router is **cisco**.

Objective

- Configure an ISDN router to make a successful connection to a local ISDN switch.

Background/Preparation

This lab assumes that a router with an ISDN BRI U interface is available. An Adtran Atlas550 ISDN emulator is used to simulate the ISDN switch and cloud. If an ISDN router is not available, review the lab and perform as many noninterface commands as possible.

Cable a network that is similar to the one in Figure 4-1. You can use any router that meets the interface requirements in Figure 4-1 (that is, 800, 1600, 1700, 2500, and 2600 routers, or a combination). See the information in Appendix C, "Router Interface Summary Chart," to correctly specify the interface identifiers based on the equipment in your lab. The 1721 series routers produced the configuration output in this lab. Another router might produce slightly different output. Execute the following tasks on each router unless you are specifically instructed otherwise.

Start a HyperTerminal session.

Implement the procedure documented in Appendix E, "Erasing and Reloading the Router," on all routers before you continue with this lab.

Task 1: Configure the Router

Configure the hostname, console, vty, and enable passwords according to Table 4-1.

Task 2: Verify the ISDN BRI Switch Type

Not all ISDN switch types are the same worldwide, so the first step is to configure the ISDN TE1 device (the router) to tell it what ISDN switch type is in use. The ISDN telco provider provides this information. In this case, the ISDN switch type, which the Adtran simulator supports, is National ISDN-1 (North America) and is configured on the router using the keyword **basic-ni**. To check the ISDN BRI status, issue the following command before you issue configuration commands:

```
Ottawa#show isdn status
```

What is the Layer 1 status? _____

What is the ISDN switch type? _____

Task 3: Specify the Switch Type

Step 1.   To specify the ISDN switch type, use the **isdn switch-type** command at the global configuration mode prompt. You can review the different switch types that are available by using the **isdn switch-type ?** command:

```
Ottawa#configure terminal
Ottawa(config)#isdn switch-type ?
```

How many different switch types are available? ___

Step 2.   To configure the router to communicate with a National ISDN-1 switch type, enter the following:

```
Ottawa(config)#isdn switch-type basic-ni
```

Task 4: Verify the Switch Status

Check the state of the ISDN interface again:

```
Ottawa#show isdn status
```

What is the Layer 1 status? _____

What is the ISDN switch type? _____

Task 5: Activate the BRI Connection

Activate the ISDN BRI by using the **no shutdown** command at the interface configuration prompt:

```
Ottawa#configure terminal
Ottawa(config)#interface bri 0
Ottawa(config-if)#no shutdown
```

Task 6: Review the Switch Status

At this stage, the ISDN BRI should be physically active, and one TEI should be negotiated. Enter the following command to review the switch status:

```
Ottawa#show isdn status
```

What is the Layer 1 status? _____

What is the ISDN switch type? _____

Has the Layer 2 status changed? _____

Task 7: Configure the ISDN SPIDs

Depending on the region, you might have to specify ISDN SPIDs for the ISDN switch to respond to the ISDN TE1 correctly. The SPIDs that the Adtran simulator supports are specified as **isdn spid1** and **isdn spid2**. To configure the SPIDs, issue the following commands:

```
Ottawa(config)#interface bri 0
Ottawa(config-if)#isdn spid1 51055510000001 5551000
Ottawa(config-if)#isdn spid2 51055510010001 5551001
```

Task 8: Review the Switch Status

Check the state of the ISDN interface again:

```
Ottawa#show isdn status
```

What does the output specify about SPID1?

_____

_____

What does the output specify about SPID2?

_____

_____

If you examine this output carefully, you will see that the assigned SPID values have not been sent to the ISDN switch and have not been verified. This is because you specified them after the ISDN interface was enabled. To send the SPID values, you must reset the interface.

Task 9: Reset the Interface

To manually reset the ISDN BRI interface, issue the command **clear interface bri 0**. This command causes all ISDN parameters to be renegotiated. Issue the **clear** command on the router, and then check the ISDN interface status. SPID1 and SPID2 are sent and validated:

```
Ottawa#clear interface bri 0
Ottawa#show isdn status
```

Have SPID1 and SPID2 been sent and verified? _____

Task 10: Save the Configuration and Reboot

Save the configuration and reboot the router. This time, verify that the ISDN interface has correctly negotiated with the ISDN switch. Review activity on the ISDN interface by using the **show isdn active** command:

```
Ottawa#copy running-config startup-config
Ottawa#reload
```

```
Ottawa#show isdn active
```

The history table has a maximum of how many entries? _____

The history table data is retained for how long? _____

After you complete the previous tasks, log off (by entering **exit**) and turn the router off. Then, remove and store the cables and adapter.

Curriculum Lab 4-2: Configuring Legacy DDR (4.3.2)

Figure 4-2   Topology for Lab 4-2

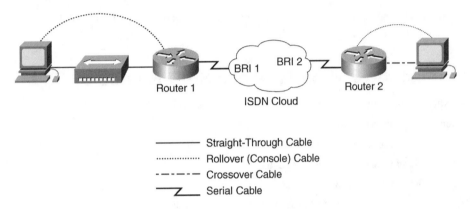

———— Straight-Through Cable
.... Rollover (Console) Cable
– – – – – Crossover Cable
⌐Z⌐ Serial Cable

Table 4-2   Lab Equipment Configuration

Router Designation	Router Name	Fast Ethernet0 Address/Subnet Mask	SPID Numbers	Phone Numbers	Adtran Connection
Router 1	Tokyo	192.168.1.1/24	51055510000001 51055510010001	5551000 5551001	BRI 1
Router 2	Moscow	192.168.2.1/24	51055520000001 51055520010001	5552000 5552001	BRI 2

The enable secret password for both routers is **class**.

The enable, vty, and console password for both routers is **cisco**.

Objectives

- Configure an ISDN router to make a legacy DDR call to another ISDN-capable router.

- When the DDR connection is made successfully, augment the configuration to specify that only HTTP traffic will bring up the link.

Background/Preparation

In this lab, two ISDN routers are required. If ISDN routers are not available, review the lab to become familiar with the process. An Adtran Atlas550 ISDN emulator is used to simulate the switch/ISDN cloud.

Cable a network that is similar to the one in Figure 4-2. You can use any router that meets the interface requirements in Figure 4-2 (that is, 800, 1600, 1700, 2500, and 2600 routers, or a combination). See the information in Appendix C to correctly specify the interface identifiers based on the equipment in your lab. The 1721 series routers produced the configuration output in this lab. Another router might produce slightly different output. Execute the following tasks on each router unless you are specifically instructed otherwise.

Start a HyperTerminal session.

Implement the procedure documented in Appendix E on all routers before you continue with this lab.

Task 1: Configure the Router

Configure the hostname, console, vty, and enable passwords according to Table 4-2. If you have difficulty doing this, see Lab 1-1, "Configuring NAT."

Task 2: Define the Switch Type and SPID Numbers

You must specify the switch type and SPID numbers on the routers:

```
Router(config)#hostname Tokyo
Tokyo(config)#enable secret class
Tokyo(config)#isdn switch-type basic-ni
Tokyo(config)#interface fastethernet 0
Tokyo(config-if)#ip address 192.168.1.1 255.255.255.0
Tokyo(config-if)#no shutdown
Tokyo(config-if)#exit
Tokyo(config)#interface bri 0
Tokyo(config-if)#isdn spid1 51055510000001 5551000
Tokyo(config-if)#isdn spid2 51055510010001 5551001
Tokyo(config-if)#no shutdown
```

```
Router(config)# hostname Moscow
Moscow(config)# enable secret class
Moscow(config)# isdn switch-type basic-ni
Moscow(config)# interface fastethernet 0
Moscow(config-if)#ip address 192.168.2.1 255.255.255.0
Moscow(config-if)#no shutdown
Moscow(config-if)#exit
Moscow(config)# interface bri 0
Moscow(config-if)#isdn spid1 51055520000001 5552000
Moscow(config-if)#isdn spid2 51055520010001 5552001
Moscow(config-if)#no shutdown
```

Task 3: Define the Static Routes for DDR

Step 1.   Use static and default routes rather than dynamic routing so that you can reduce the cost of the dialup connection. To configure a static route, you must know the network address of the network to be reached and the IP address of the next router on the path to this destination:

```
Moscow#configure terminal
Moscow(config)#ip route 192.168.1.0 255.255.255.0 192.168.3.1
```

```
Tokyo#configure terminal
Tokyo(config)#ip route 0.0.0.0 0.0.0.0 192.168.3.2
```

Step 2.   Execute the **show ip route** command to verify that the routes exist.

Task 4: Specify Interesting Traffic for DDR

Specify the traffic that will cause the DDR interface to dial up the remote router. For the moment, declare that all IP traffic is "interesting." You do this by using the **dialer-list** command:

```
Tokyo#configure terminal
Tokyo(config)#dialer-list 1 protocol ip permit
Tokyo(config)#interface bri 0
Tokyo(config-if)#dialer-group 1
Tokyo(config-if)#end
```

Task 5: Configure the DDR Dialer Information for Router 1

Step 1.   Configure the correct dialer information necessary for the correct function of the dialer profile and dialer interface. This includes IP address information, PPP configuration, name, passwords, and dial number:

```
Tokyo#configure terminal
Tokyo(config)#interface bri 0
Tokyo(config-if)#ip address 192.168.3.1 255.255.255.0
```

Step 2.   Configure the PPP information:

```
Tokyo#configure terminal
Tokyo(config)#username Moscow password class
Tokyo(config)#interface bri 0
Tokyo(config-if)#encapsulation ppp
Tokyo(config-if)#ppp authentication chap
```

Step 3.   Configure the dial information:

```
Tokyo#configure terminal
Tokyo(config)#interface bri 0
Tokyo(config-if)#dialer idle-timeout 120
Tokyo(config-if)#dialer map ip 192.168.3.2 name Moscow 5552000
```

Task 6: Configure the DDR Dialer Information for Router 2

```
Moscow#configure terminal
Moscow(config)#dialer-list 1 protocol ip permit
Moscow(config)#username Tokyo password class
Moscow(config)#interface bri 0
Moscow(config-if)#ip address 192.168.3.2 255.255.255.0
Moscow(config-if)#dialer-group 1
Moscow(config-if)#encapsulation ppp
Moscow(config-if)#ppp authentication chap
Moscow(config-if)#dialer idle-timeout 120
Moscow(config-if)#dialer map ip 192.168.3.1 name Tokyo 5551000
```

Task 7: View the Tokyo Router Configuration

To view the configuration, use the **show running-config** command:

```
Tokyo#show running-config
```

What authentication is being used? _____

What are the ISDN SPIDs on the Tokyo router?

_____

Task 8: Verify the DDR Configuration

Step 1.   Generate some interesting traffic across the DDR link from the remote Moscow router to verify that connections are made correctly:

```
Tokyo#ping 192.168.2.1
```

Did the pings succeed? _____

Step 2.   If not, troubleshoot the router configuration.

Step 3.   Use the **show interface** command and note that the output shows that the interface is "spoofing." This provides a mechanism for the interface to simulate an active state for internal processes, such as routing, on the router. You can also use the **show interface** command to display information about the B channel:

```
Tokyo#show interface bri 0
```

Step 4.   After you complete the previous tasks, log off (by entering **exit**) and turn the router off. Then, remove and store the cables and adapter.

Curriculum Lab 4-3: Configuring Dialer Profiles (4.3.7)

Figure 4-3   Topology for Lab 4-3

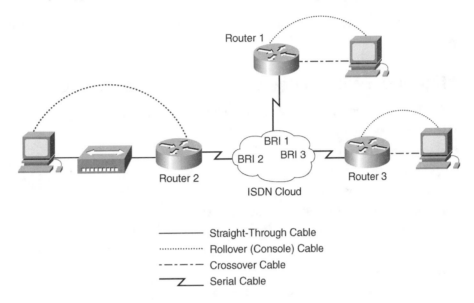

Table 4-3   Lab Equipment Configuration

Router Designation	Router Name	Fast Ethernet0 Address with Subnet Mask	SPID Numbers	Phone Numbers	Adtran Connection
Router 1	Tokyo	192.168.1.1/24	51055510000001 51055510010001	5551000 5551001	BRI 1
Router 2	Moscow	192.168.2.1/24	51055520000001 51055520010001	5552000 5552001	BRI 2
Router 3	Sydney	192.168.3.1/24	51055530000001 51055530010001	5553000 5553001	BRI 3

The enable secret password for all routers is **class**.

The enable, vty, and console password for all routers is **cisco**.

Objective

- Configure ISDN dialer profiles on the routers, enabling a DDR call to be made from two remote routers simultaneously into a central ISDN BRI router.

Background/Preparation

In this lab, three ISDN routers are required. If ISDN routers are not available, review the lab to become familiar with the process. An Adtran Atlas550 ISDN emulator is used to simulate the switch/ISDN cloud.

Cable a network that is similar to the one in Figure 4-3. You can use any router that meets the interface requirements in Figure 4-3 (that is, 800, 1600, 1700, 2500, and 2600 routers, or a combination). See the information in Appendix C to correctly specify the interface identifiers based on the equipment in your lab. The 1721 series routers produced the configuration output in this lab. Another router might produce slightly different output. Execute the following tasks on each router unless you are specifically instructed otherwise.

Start a HyperTerminal session.

Implement the procedure documented in Appendix E on all routers before you continue with this lab.

Task 1: Configure the Router

Configure the hostname, console, vty, and enable passwords according to Table 4-3. If you have difficulty doing this, see Lab 1-1, "Configuring NAT."

Task 2: Define the Switch Type and SPID Numbers

To configure the switch type and SPID numbers, use the following commands:

```
Router(config)#hostname Tokyo
Tokyo(config)#enable secret class
Tokyo(config)#isdn switch-type basic-ni
Tokyo(config)#interface fastethernet 0
Tokyo(config-if)#ip address 192.168.1.1 255.255.255.0
Tokyo(config-if)#no shutdown
Tokyo(config-if)#exit
Tokyo(config)#interface bri 0
Tokyo(config-if)#isdn spid1 51055510000001 5551000
Tokyo(config-if)#isdn spid2 51055510010001 5551001
Tokyo(config-if)#no shutdown
```

```
Router(config)#hostname Moscow
Moscow(config)#enable secret class
Moscow(config)#isdn switch-type basic-ni
Moscow(config)#interface fastethernet 0
Moscow(config-if)#ip address 192.168.2.1 255.255.255.0
Moscow(config-if)#no shutdown
Moscow(config-if)#exit
Moscow(config)#interface bri 0
Moscow(config-if)#isdn spid1 51055520000001 5552000
Moscow(config-if)#isdn spid2 51055520010001 5552001
Moscow(config-if)#no shutdown
```

```
Router(config)#hostname Sydney
Sydney(config)#enable secret class
Sydney(config)#isdn switch-type basic-ni
Sydney(config)#interface fastethernet 0
Sydney(config-if)#ip address 192.168.3.1 255.255.255.0
Sydney(config-if)#no shutdown
Sydney(config-if)#exit
Sydney(config)#interface bri 0
Sydney(config-if)#isdn spid1 51055530000001 5553000
Sydney(config-if)#isdn spid2 51055530010001 5553001
Sydney(config-if)#no shutdown
```

Task 3: Define the Static Routes for DDR

Use static and default routes rather than dynamic routing so that you can reduce the cost of the dialup connection. To configure a static route, you must know the network address of the network trying to be reached and the IP address of the next router on the path to this destination:

```
Moscow#configure terminal
Moscow(config)#ip route 0.0.0.0 0.0.0.0 192.168.253.1
```

```
Sydney#configure terminal
Sydney(config)#ip route 0.0.0.0 0.0.0.0 192.168.254.1
```

```
Tokyo#configure terminal
Tokyo(config)#ip route 192.168.2.0 255.255.255.0 192.168.253.2
Tokyo(config)#ip route 192.168.3.0 255.255.255.0 192.168.254.2
```

Task 4: Specify Interesting Traffic for DDR

You must define traffic as "interesting" to cause the DDR interface to dial up the remote router. For the moment, declare that all IP traffic is interesting by using the **dialer-list** command:

```
Moscow(config)#dialer-list 1 protocol ip permit
Moscow(config)#interface dialer 0
Moscow(config-if)#dialer-group 1
```

```
Sydney(config)#dialer-list 1 protocol ip permit
Sydney(config)#interface dialer 0
Sydney(config-if)#dialer-group 1
```

```
Tokyo#configure terminal
Tokyo(config)#dialer-list 1 protocol ip permit
Tokyo(config)#interface dialer 1
Tokyo(config-if)#description The Profile for the Moscow router
Tokyo(config-if)#dialer-group 1
Tokyo(config-if)#interface dialer 2
Tokyo(config-if)#description The Profile for the Sydney router
Tokyo(config-if)#dialer-group 1
```

Task 5: Configure the DDR Dialer Information

Configure the correct dialer information that is necessary for the correct function of the dialer profile and dialer interface. This includes IP address information, PPP configuration, name, passwords, and dial number:

```
Tokyo(config)#interface dialer 1
Tokyo(config-if)#ip address 192.168.253.1 255.255.255.0
Tokyo(config-if)#interface dialer 2
Tokyo(config-if)#ip address 192.168.254.1 255.255.255.0
Tokyo(config-if)#interface bri 0
```

```
Tokyo(config-if)#encapsulation ppp
Tokyo(config-if)#ppp authentication chap
Tokyo(config-if)#interface dialer 1
Tokyo(config-if)#encapsulation ppp
Tokyo(config-if)#ppp authentication chap
Tokyo(config-if)#interface dialer 2
Tokyo(config-if)#encapsulation ppp
Tokyo(config-if)#ppp authentication chap
Tokyo(config-if)#exit
Tokyo(config)#username Moscow password class
Tokyo(config)#username Sydney password class
```

```
Moscow(config)#interface dialer 0
Moscow(config-if)#ip address 192.168.253.2 255.255.255.0
Moscow(config-if)#interface bri 0
Moscow(config-if)#encapsulation ppp
Moscow(config-if)#ppp authentication chap
Moscow(config-if)#interface dialer 0
Moscow(config-if)#encapsulation ppp
Moscow(config-if)#ppp authentication chap
Moscow(config-if)#no shutdown
Moscow(config-if)#exit
Moscow(config)#username Tokyo password class
```

```
Sydney(config)#interface dialer 0
Sydney(config-if)#ip address 192.168.254.2 255.255.255.0
Sydney(config-if)#interface bri 0
Sydney(config-if)#encapsulation ppp
Sydney(config-if)#ppp authentication chap
Sydney(config-if)#interface dialer 0
Sydney(config-if)#encapsulation ppp
Sydney(config-if)#ppp authentication chap
Sydney(config-if)#no shutdown
Sydney(config-if)#exit
Sydney(config)#username Tokyo password class
```

Task 6: Configure the Dialer Information

Next, you must configure the dial information to specify the remote name of the remote router in the dialer profile, and the dial string (phone number) to use to contact this remote device. Use the commands in the following steps to do this.

Step 1.   To configure the dial information on Tokyo, use the following:

```
Tokyo(config)#interface dialer 1
Tokyo(config-if)#dialer remote-name Moscow
Tokyo(config-if)#dialer string 5552000
```

```
Tokyo(config-if)#dialer string 5552001
Tokyo(config-if)#interface dialer 2
Tokyo(config-if)#dialer remote-name Sydney
Tokyo(config-if)#dialer string 5553000
Tokyo(config-if)#dialer string 5553001
```

Step 2. To configure the dial information on Moscow, use the following:

```
Moscow(config-if)#interface dialer 0
Moscow(config-if)#dialer remote-name Tokyo
Moscow(config-if)#dialer string 5551000
Moscow(config-if)#dialer string 5551001
```

Step 3. To configure the dial information on Sydney, use the following:

```
Sydney(config-if)#interface dialer 0
Sydney(config-if)#dialer remote-name Tokyo
Sydney(config-if)#dialer string 5551000
Sydney(config-if)#dialer string 5551001
```

Task 7: Associate the Dialer Profiles

Finally, associate the dialer profiles with the dialer interfaces that will be used, when needed. Create a dialer pool and put the interfaces and the associated dialer profiles in a common pool. The commands for doing this are as follows.

Step 1. On Tokyo, the commands issued would be as follows:

```
Tokyo(config-if)#interface bri 0
Tokyo(config-if)#dialer pool-member 1
Tokyo(config-if)#interface dialer 1
Tokyo(config-if)#dialer pool 1
Tokyo(config-if)#interface dialer 2
Tokyo(config-if)#dialer pool 1
```

Step 2. On Moscow, the commands issued would be as follows:

```
Moscow(config-if)#interface bri 0
Moscow(config-if)#dialer pool-member 1
Moscow(config-if)#interface dialer 0
Moscow(config-if)#dialer pool 1
```

Step 3. Use the same commands to configure the Sydney router.

Task 8: Configure the Dialer Timeouts

Step 1. Configure a **dialer idle-timeout** of 60 seconds for each of the dialer interfaces:

```
Tokyo(config)#interface dialer 1
Tokyo(config-if)#dialer idle-timeout 60
Tokyo(config-if)#interface dialer 2
Tokyo(config-if)#dialer idle-timeout 60
```

Step 2. Repeat these commands on Moscow and Sydney.

Task 9: View the Tokyo Router Configuration

To view the configuration, use the **show running-config** command:

Tokyo#**show running-config**

How many username statements exist? _____

What authentication type is being used for PPP? _____

Which sections of the configuration list the authentication type? _____

What are the dialer strings on the Tokyo router?

_____

_____

_____

_____

_____

_____

Task 10: Verify the DDR Configuration

Step 1.   Generate some interesting traffic across the DDR link from Moscow and Sydney to verify that connections are made correctly and that the dialer profiles are functioning:

Moscow#**ping 192.168.1.1**

Sydney#**ping 192.168.1.1**

Did the pings succeed? _____

Step 2.   If not, troubleshoot the router configurations.

What other information was displayed when the ping was issued?

_____

_____

_____

_____

Step 3.   Use the **show dialer** command to see the reason for the call. This information is shown for each channel:

Tokyo#**show dialer**

Which dialer strings are associated with Dialer1? _____

What is the last status for dial string 5553000 in the Dialer2 readout? _____

Step 4.   Use the **show interface** command and note that the output shows that the interface is "spoofing." This provides a mechanism for the interface to simulate an active state for internal processes, such as routing, on the router. You can also use the **show interface** command to display information about the B channel:

Tokyo#**show interface bri 0**

After you complete the previous tasks, log off (by entering **exit**) and turn the router off. Then, remove and store the cables and adapter.

Challenge Lab 4-4: Configuring Dialer Maps and Dialer Profiles

You are hired as a consultant for a company that has three remote locations: Mo, Larry, and Curley. The task at hand is to set up ISDN across their WAN and the addressing on their internal network. The company wants you to use dialer maps on the Larry and Curley routers pointing to the Mo router. The Mo router will use dialer profiles pointing to the Larry and Curley routers.

This lab challenges your ability to configure dialer profiles and dialer maps in an ISDN environment. Figure 4-4 presents the topology for this lab.

Figure 4-4   ISDN Challenge Lab Topology

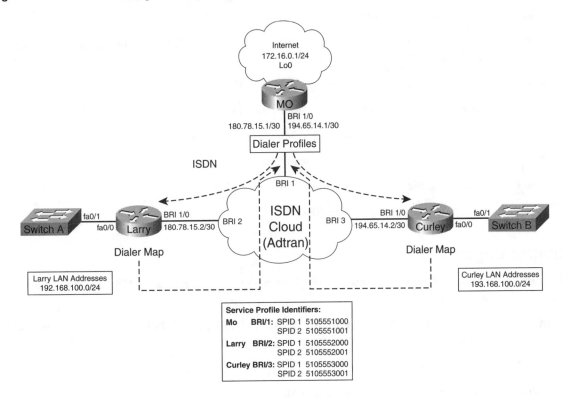

Task 1: Physical

Connect and configure the devices as shown in Figure 4-4.

Task 2: Logical Mo

Step 1.   Configure router Mo with encapsulation PPP on the BRI interface using CHAP authentication and Multilink.

Step 2.   Configure dialer profiles.

Step 3.   Configure two dialer interfaces each using two dialer strings and given IP addresses (SPIDs remain in dialer-pool 1).

Step 4.   Configure usernames and passwords:

- Username **Larry** password **0 cisco**.

- Username **Curley** password **0 cisco**.

Step 5.   Permit both dialer lists.

Step 6.   Configure router Mo with switch type basic-ni.

Step 7.   Configure static routes to Larry and Curley dialer interfaces and to SwitchA and SwitchB LANs.

Step 8.   Create access lists permitting both switched networks and the loopback on Mo.

Task 3: Logical Larry

Step 1.   Configure Larry with encapsulation PPP on the BRI interface using CHAP authentication and Multilink.

Step 2.   Use switch type basic-ni.

Step 3.   Create dialer 0 to use the IP address 180.78.15.2 /30. Include **dialer-pool**, **dialer-group**, and **permit dialer-list**.

Step 4.   Configure Larry's BRI using the appropriate SPIDs.

Step 5.   Make sure that both B channels are used simultaneously.

Step 6.   Configure username and password to **Mo** with password **cisco**.

Step 7.   Configure interface fa0/0 on Larry with IP address 192.168.100.1 /24.

Step 8.   Configure static routes to the Curley LAN and Mo's loopback.

Step 9.   Configure a default route out of BRI1/0.

Task 4: Logical Curley

Step 1.   Configure Curley with encapsulation PPP on the BRI interface using CHAP authentication and Multilink.

Step 2.   Create dialer 0 with given IP address 194.65.14.2 /30. Include **dialer-pool**, **dialer-group**, and **permit dialer-list**.

Step 3.   Configure the BRI interface with the appropriate SPIDs.

Step 4.   Configure username and password to **Mo** with password **class**.

Step 5.   Configure interface fa0/0 with an IP address of 193.168.100.1 /24.

Step 6.   Configure static routes to the Larry LAN and to the loopback on Mo.

Step 7.   Configure a default route out of BRI 1/0.

Task 5: Switches

Configure each switch with an IP address and appropriate default gateway for its network.

Task 6: Verification

This lab is complete when you can ping every interface shown in Figure 4-4.

CHAPTER 5

Frame Relay

The Study Guide portion of this chapter uses a combination of fill-in-the-blank, multiple-choice, and open-ended question exercises to test your knowledge of the theory of Frame Relay terminology, bandwidth, and flow control. This chapter also discusses the importance of Frame Relay addressing, map statements, and the use of Inverse Address Resolution Protocol (ARP) and Local Management Interface (LMI) operation.

The Lab Exercises portion of this chapter includes all the online curriculum labs and three challenge labs to ensure that you have mastered the practical, hands-on skills needed for Frame Relay maps, subinterface configuration, and troubleshooting.

Study Guide

Frame Relay Concepts

Frame Relay is a standalone packet-switched technology that operates using virtual circuits to connect LANs across a cloud. It uses switched virtual circuits (SVCs) (less common) and permanent virtual circuits (PVCs), which the carrier preconfigures, to join locations. Frame Relay also provides no error-checking technology, because it was designed to run on digital, high-quality lines. A Frame Relay edge router may have multiple PVCs toward different locations and labels each one with a data-link connection identifier (DLCI). Each PVC has its own set amount of bandwidth inside the cloud; this is called the committed information rate (CIR), which is the method of flow control for Frame Relay. Commonly, Frame Relay networks are set up in either star (hub-and-spoke), Frame Relay star, full-mesh, or partial-mesh topologies. In a star topology, all the edge routers connect to a central location, as opposed to a Frame Relay star, where the edge routers connect to a cloud. Mesh and partial-mesh topologies connect every location, or at least most of them, to one another. Local Management Interfaces (LMI) extensions are also provided with Frame Relay to reduce the transfer delay between two locations. LMIs include mechanisms to keep track of keepalive messages and VC status and a mechanism with flow control; LMI types are Cisco, Q933a, and ANSI. LMIs combined with Inverse ARP allow a router to associate a DLCI with a network layer address; this allows the router to learn PVCs dynamically.

Concept Questions

1. Compare a PVC to an SVC.

   _____

   _____

   _____

   _____

   _____

2. LMI is a signaling standard that allows DTEs to dynamically acquire information about a network's status. Keepalive messages are one example of status messages that are sent. Explain how routers use keepalive messages.

   _____

   _____

3. Explain how a DLCI is used to route Frame Relay traffic.

   _____

   _____

   _____

Configuring Frame Relay

To configure Frame Relay, go into the serial interface connected to the frame cloud or frame switch and enter **encapsulation frame-relay** [**cisco** | **ietf**]. **cisco** is the default encapsulation and should be used only if you're connecting to another Cisco router. You should use the **ietf** encapsulation option when connecting non-Cisco routers.

You can also set the LMI type with the command **frame-relay lmi-type** [**cisco** | **q933a** | **ansi**]. This is not necessary for Cisco IOS Software Release 11.2 and later, because LMI types are automatically discovered.

You might need to statically configure a Frame Relay map with the command **frame-relay map** [*protocol*] [*network address*] [**dlci**] **broadcast** when Inverse ARP is not available on the router. The **broadcast** keyword allows routing updates to be sent across the cloud. The use of a subinterface enables you to use one interface to connect multiple locations, avoiding the need to purchase more equipment. Each subinterface can be set up as a point-to-point or point-to-multipoint interface (**interface serial** [*number*]/ [*number*].[*subinterface number*] [**point-to-point** | **point-to-multipoint**]). Point-to-point is used when each subinterface will act as point-to-point connection to another interface. The subinterfaces must also be on the same subnet, separate from others. A point-to-multipoint interface is used when connecting multiple locations. In this case, all connecting interfaces must be on the same subnet. To verify the configurations, you can use the **show frame-relay map** and **show frame-relay pvc** commands to display PVC information. To clear out any dynamically learned maps, use the command **clear frame-relay inarp**.

Concept Questions

1. Explain why using subinterfaces resolves the split-horizon issue without your having to disable the feature.

2. Forward explicit congestion notification (FECN) and backward explicit congestion notification (BECN) are used for traffic shaping. Explain each one's purpose and how they are used to notify devices of congestion.

3. You are troubleshooting a Frame Relay network that is not functioning. What commands can you use to determine the cause of the problem, and what information do these commands display?

Chapter Review Questions

For multiple-choice questions 1 through 20, circle the correct answers. Some questions have more than one answer.

1. Which of the following are valid Frame Relay LMI types? (Select three)

   A. Cisco

   B. Q921

   C. Q931

   D. Q933a

   E. ANSI

   F. IETF

   G. Annex A

   H. Annex D

2. Which of the following are true of point-to-point subinterfaces? (Select all that apply)

   A. They are used to establish one PVC connection.

   B. They are used to establish multiple PVC connections.

   C. Each pair of point-to-point routers requires its own subnet.

   D. All participating interfaces are in the same subnet.

   E. The split-horizon rule does not apply to routing update traffic.

3. DLCI numbers range from 0 through 1023. What range of numbers is available to subscribers?

   A. 0–1023

   B. 1–15 and 1008–1022

   C. 992–1007

   D. 16–991

4. When a Frame Relay switch notices its queue increasing, what does it use to reduce the flow of frames it receives?

   A. Explicit correction notifications

   B. Error correction notifications

   C. Explicit congestion notifications

   D. Error congestion notifications

5. What command enables you to configure the local DLCI on the subinterface?

   A. Router(config)#**frame-relay interface dlci** [*number*]

   B. Router(config-if)#**frame-relay interface dlci** [*number*]

   C. Router(config)#**frame relay interface-dlci** [*number*]

   D. Router(config-subif)#**frame-relay interface-dlci** [*number*]

6. Which of the following are true of the Local Management Interface? (Select all that apply)

   A. Cisco IOS Software Release 11.2 or later allows the router to automatically determine the LMI type used by the switch.

   B. It is used between the DCE and the Frame switch in the carrier's network.

   C. It is used between the DTE and the Frame switch in the carrier's network.

   D. It can be used only with Inverse ARP enabled.

7. Which of the following are displayed when you use the command **show frame-relay lmi**? (Select two)

   A. LMI type

   B. DLCI number

   C. The number of status messages sent and received between the router and the Frame switch

   D. Current map entries and their status

   E. The number of status messages sent and received for each configured PVC

8. When you configure Frame Relay subinterfaces, which of the following must *not* be configured?

   A. Frame Relay encapsulation on the physical interface

   B. The DLCI numbers on the subinterface

   C. The subinterface type as multipoint

   D. The IP address on the physical interface

   E. The IP address on the subinterface

9. What would be the result if the **broadcast** keyword at the end of the following command line were omitted?

   ```
   frame-relay map ip 131.108.123.1 100 broadcast
   ```

   A. Routing updates would be forwarded.

   B. Routing updates would not be forwarded.

   C. The statement would be broadcast to all other routers in the frame network.

   D. The router would be prevented from becoming a broadcast firewall.

10. Which of the following solve the split-horizon quandary in a Frame Relay environment with multiple connections over a single physical interface? (Select two)

    A. Partial-mesh topology

    B. Full-mesh topology

    C. Subinterfaces

    D. Point-to-point topology

11. Which of the following are true of multipoint subinterfaces? (Select all that apply)

    A. They are used to establish one PVC connection.

    B. They are used to establish multiple PVC connections.

    C. Each pair of point-to-point routers requires its own subnet.

    D. All participating interfaces are in the same subnet.

    E. The split-horizon rule does not apply to routing update traffic.

    F. The split-horizon rule is applied because the subinterface acts like an NBMA interface.

12. What two methods allow a router to associate network layer and data link layer addresses?

    A. Inverse ARP with LMI messages

    B. Inverse RARP

    C. Reverse ARP

    D. Frame Relay map

    E. DLCI status messages

    F. FECN

    G. BECN

13. What is used to distinguish between various PVCs on a single line?

    A. LMI

    B. LAPF

    C. DLCI

    D. LAPD

14. What are DLCI 0 and DLCI 1023 reserved for?

    A. Cisco LMI type is 0, and Q933a LMI type is 1023.

    B. Q933a LMI type is 0, and Cisco LMI type is 1023.

    C. Cisco LMI type is 0, and Q931 LMI type is 1023.

    D. IETF LMI type is 0, and Cisco LMI type is 1023.

15. Which of the following are true of DLCI values? (Select three)

    A. They have local significance.

    B. They have global significance.

    C. They are unique to the physical channel on which they reside.

    D. Different DLCI values can be used at each end to refer to the same VC.

    E. DLCI values must be the same on each end when referring to the same VC.

16. How does a switch identify frames that exceed the CIR?

    A. DE

    B. FECN

    C. BECN

    D. LAPF

17. What are the possible connection states that a VC could be in when using the **show frame-relay pvc** command? (Select three)

    A. Active

    B. Passive

    C. Inactive

    D. Deleted

    E. Unknown

18. When configuring Frame Relay, what can you do to prevent split-horizon problems? (Select two)

    A. Use a physical interface to route traffic for multiple PVCs.

    B. Configure a separate subinterface for each PVC.

    C. Configure a separate subinterface for multiple PVCs.

    D. Disable split horizon.

19. Most ISPs disable the use of Inverse ARP in their networks. What command is the alternative solution when they cannot be dynamically mapped?

    A. frame-relay inverse-arp

    B. frame-relay map

    C. frame-relay interface-type

    D. frame-relay ip map

20. Which of the following appear when you use the **show frame-relay pvc** command? (Select all that apply)

    A. Status of each configured connection

    B. Traffic statistics

    C. IP address of the remote location

    D. Map entries

    E. The number of FECN and BECN entries received by the router

Lab Exercises

Curriculum Lab 5-1: Configuring Frame Relay (5.2.1)

Figure 5-1   Topology for Lab 5-1

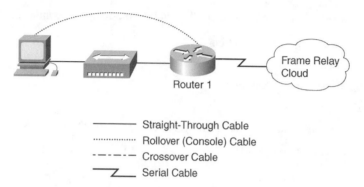

Router 1

———————— Straight-Through Cable
················ Rollover (Console) Cable
– – – – – Crossover Cable
‾‾Z‾‾‾ Serial Cable

Table 5-1   Lab Equipment Configuration

Router Designation	Router Name	Fast Ethernet 0 Address/Subnet Mask	Adtran Connection
Router 1	Cork	192.168.14.1/24	1/1

The enable secret password for this router is **class**.

The enable, vty, and console password for this router is **cisco**.

Objective

- Configure a router to establish a connection to a local Frame Relay switch.

Background/Preparation

This lab uses an Adtran Atlas550 Frame Relay to simulate the Frame Relay switch/cloud.

The Cork Wholesale Food Company has just had a Frame Relay circuit installed to its local central office (CO) by the telco carrier. The network administrator must confirm that the router and Frame Relay switch can communicate successfully.

Cable a network that is similar to the one in Figure 5-1. You can use any router that meets the interface requirements in Figure 5-1 (that is, 800, 1600, 1700, 2500, and 2600 routers, or a combination). See the information in Appendix C, "Router Interface Summary Chart," to correctly specify the interface identifiers based on the equipment in your lab. The 1721 series routers produced the configuration output in this lab. Another router might produce slightly different output. Execute the following tasks on each router unless you are specifically instructed otherwise.

Start a HyperTerminal session.

Implement the procedure documented in Appendix E, "Erasing and Reloading the Router," on all routers before you continue with this lab.

Task 1: Configure the Routers

Configure the hostname, console, vty, and enable passwords according to Table 5-1. If you have difficulty doing this, see Lab 1-1, "Configuring NAT."

Task 2: Configure the Serial Interface

Step 1.   In Frame Relay, the customer router is considered to be the DTE device. To configure the serial interface, you must define the Layer 2 Frame Relay frame type. To configure the frame type, use the following commands:

```
Cork#configure terminal
Cork(config)#interface serial 0
Cork(config-if)#encapsulation frame-relay IETF
```

Step 2.   Next, you need to configure the format of the Frame Relay management protocol. To configure the Local Management Interface (LMI) type, use the following commands:

```
Cork(config-if)#frame-relay lmi-type ansi
Cork(config-if)#no shutdown
Cork(config-if)#ctrl+z
```

Task 3: Verify the Frame Relay Configuration

To verify the configuration, use the **show interface** commands that are related to Frame Relay. To view the serial interface configuration, enter the following command:

```
Cork#show interface serial 0
```

What is the state of the interface? Serial 0 is ___, line protocol is ___.

What is the encapsulation type? _____

What state is the DTE LMI in? _____

What is the LMI type? _____

Task 4: Review Switch Assignments

To verify that the DLCIs are defined on the switch, use **show frame-relay pvc**. The DLCIs are learned by the router via LMI and can be viewed:

```
Cork#show frame-relay pvc
```

What DLCI numbers are available on the switch? _____

What is the PVC status of the first DLCI? _____

Task 5: Check the Frame Relay Map

The output from the **show frame-relay map** command shows that none of the DLCIs defined on the switch are in use. The PVC is inactive, and there is no current mapping between the Layer 2 DLCI and Layer 3 IP address.

Why is this?

_____

After you complete the previous tasks, log off (by entering **exit**) and turn the router off. Then, remove and store the cables and adapter.

Curriculum Lab 5-2: Configuring Frame Relay PVC (5.2.2)

Figure 5-2   Topology for Lab 5-2

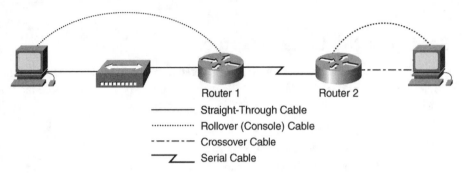

Router 1   Router 2

—————— Straight-Through Cable

················ Rollover (Console) Cable

----- Crossover Cable

⎯Z⎯ Serial Cable

Table 5-2   Lab Equipment Configuration

Router Designation	Router Name	Interface Type	Serial 0 Address/Subnet Mask	Fast Ethernet 0 Address/Subnet Mask	DLCI Number
Router 1	Washington	DCE	192.168.1.1/24	192.168.3.1/24	102
Router 2	Dublin	DTE	192.168.1.2/24	192.168.2.1/24	102

The enable secret password for both routers is **class**.

The enable, vty, and console password for both routers is **cisco**.

Objective

- Configure two routers back to back as a Frame Relay PVC. You will do this manually, in the absence of a Frame Relay switch, so there will be no LMI.

Background/Preparation

Cable a network that is similar to the one in Figure 5-2. You can use any router that meets the interface requirements in Figure 5-2 (that is, 800, 1600, 1700, 2500, and 2600 routers, or a combination). See the information in Appendix C to correctly specify the interface identifiers based on the equipment in your lab. The 1721 series routers produced the configuration output in this lab. Another router might produce slightly different output. Execute the following tasks on each router unless you are specifically instructed otherwise.

Start a HyperTerminal session.

Implement the procedure documented in Appendix E on all routers before you continue with this lab.

Task 1: Configure the Routers

Configure the hostname, console, vty, and enable passwords according to Table 5-2. If you have difficulty doing this, see Lab 1-1, "Configuring NAT."

Task 2: Configure the Washington Serial Interface

First, define the Frame Relay frame type to be used on this link. To configure the encapsulation type, use the command **encapsulation frame-relay ietf**. Disable keepalive messages because there is no Frame Relay switch in this configuration (and consequently no Frame Relay DCE):

```
Washington#configure terminal

Washington(config-if)#interface serial 0

Washington(config-if)#encapsulation frame-relay ietf
```

```
Washington(config-if)#no keepalive
Washington(config-if)#ip address 192.168.1.1 255.255.255.0
Washington(config-if)#no shutdown
```

Task 3: Configure the Frame Relay Map on Washington

When you are sending an Ethernet frame to a remote IP address, you must discover the remote MAC address so that you can construct the correct frame type. Frame Relay needs a similar mapping.

The remote IP address needs to be mapped to the local DLCI (Layer 2 address) so that the correctly addressed frame can be created locally for this PVC. Because you cannot map the DLCI automatically, with LMI disabled, you must create this map manually by using the **frame-relay map** command. The **broadcast** parameter allows IP broadcasts to use the same mapping for crossing this PVC:

```
Washington(config-if)#frame-relay map ip 192.168.1.2 102 ietf broadcast
```

Task 4: Configure the DCE on Washington

In this configuration using DCE cables, a clock signal is necessary. The **bandwidth** command is optional, but it is a wise choice for verifying bandwidth transmission. Another option is to describe the connection by using the **description** command. This is useful so that you can record information about the PVC, such as a remote contact person and the leased-line circuit identifier:

```
Washington(config-if)#clockrate 64000
Washington(config-if)#bandwidth 64
Washington(config-if)#description PVC to Dublin, DLCI 102, Circuit #DASS465875, Contact
John Tobin (061-8886745)
```

Task 5: Configure the Dublin Router

Configure the Dublin router by using the following commands:

```
Dublin#configure terminal
Dublin(config-if)#interface serial 0
Dublin(config-if)#encapsulation frame-relay ietf
Dublin(config-if)#no keepalive
Dublin(config-if)#no shutdown
Dublin(config-if)#ip address 192.168.1.2 255.255.255.0
Dublin(config-if)#frame-relay map ip 192.168.1.1 102 ietf broadcast
Dublin(config-if)#bandwidth 64
Dublin(config-if)#description PVC to Washington, DLCI 102, Circuit #DASS465866 Contact
Pat White (091-6543211)
```

Task 6: Verify the Frame Relay PVC

On the Washington router, enter the command **show frame-relay pvc**:

```
Washington#show frame-relay pvc
```

What DLCI number is reported? _____

What is the PVC status? _____

What is the value of the DLCI USAGE? _____

Task 7: Display the Frame Relay Map

To view the Layer 2 to Layer 3 mapping, use the **show frame-relay map** command at the privileged EXEC mode prompt:

```
Washington#show frame-relay map
```

What is the IP address shown? _____

In what state is interface serial 0? _____

Task 8: Verify Frame Relay Connectivity

Step 1.   From the Washington router, ping the Dublin router serial interface:

Did the ping succeed? _____

Step 2.   If not, troubleshoot router configurations.

After you complete the previous tasks, log off (by entering **exit**) and turn the router off. Then, remove and store the cables and adapter.

Curriculum Lab 5-3: Configuring Frame Relay Subinterfaces (5.2.5)

Figure 5-3   Topology for Lab 5-3

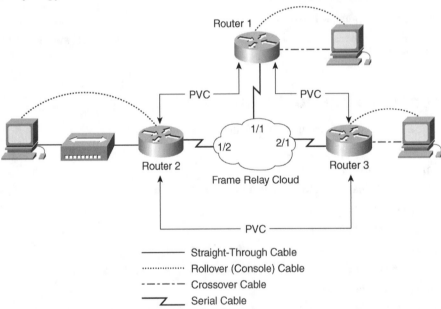

Table 5-3   Lab Equipment Configuration

Router Designation	Router Name	Interface Type	Serial 0 Address/Subnet Mask	DLCI Number	Fast Ethernet 0 Address/Subnet
Router 1	Amsterdam	DTE	192.168.4.1/24 192.168.5.1/24	102 103	192.168.1.1/24
Router 2	Paris	DTE	192.168.4.2/24 192.168.6.1/24	201 203	192.168.2.1/24
Router 3	Berlin	DTE	192.168.5.2/24 192.168.6.2/24	301 302	192.168.3.1/24

The enable secret password for all routers is **class**.

The enable, vty, and console password for all routers is **cisco**.

The routing protocol for all routers is IGRP 100.

Objective

- Configure three routers in a full-mesh Frame Relay network.

Background/Preparation

This lab uses an Adtran Atlas550 Frame Relay to simulate the switch/Frame Relay cloud.

Cable a network that is similar to the one in Figure 5-3. You can use any router that meets the interface requirements in Figure 5-3 (that is, 800, 1600, 1700, 2500, and 2600 routers, or a combination). See the information in Appendix C to correctly specify the interface identifiers based on the equipment in your lab. The 1721 series routers produced the configuration output in this lab. Another router might produce slightly different output. Execute the following tasks on each router unless you are specifically instructed otherwise.

Start a HyperTerminal session.

Implement the procedure documented in Appendix E on all routers before you continue with this lab.

Task 1: Configure the Routers

Configure the hostname, console, vty, and enable passwords according to Table 5-3. If you have difficulty doing this, see Lab 1-1, "Configuring NAT."

Task 2: Configure the Serial 0 Interfaces

Step 1.   Define the Frame Relay encapsulation type to be used on this link by using the following commands:

```
Amsterdam#configure terminal
Amsterdam(config)#interface serial 0
Amsterdam(config-if)#encapsulation frame-relay ietf
Amsterdam(config-if)#frame-relay lmi-type ansi
```

Step 2.   Use a description field to store relevant information, such as the circuit number, if you have to report a line fault:

```
Amsterdam(config-if)#description Circuit #KPN465555
Amsterdam(config-if)#no shutdown
```

Step 3.   The same commands are used to configure the Berlin and Paris routers:

```
Paris(config)#interface serial 0
Paris(config-if)#encapsulation frame-relay ietf
Paris(config-if)#frame-relay lmi-type ansi
Paris(config-if)#description Circuit #FRT372826
Paris(config-if)#no shutdown

Berlin(config)#interface serial 0
Berlin(config-if)#encapsulation frame-relay ietf
Berlin(config-if)#frame-relay lmi-type ansi
Berlin(config-if)#description Circuit #DTK465866
Berlin(config-if)#no shutdown
```

Task 3: Create Subinterfaces on the Amsterdam Router

For each of the PVCs, create a subinterface on the serial port. This subinterface will be a point-to-point configuration. For consistency and future troubleshooting, use the DLCI number as the subinterface number. The commands to create a subinterface are as follows:

```
Amsterdam(config-if)#interface serial 0.102 point-to-point

Amsterdam(config-if)#description PVC to Paris, DLCI 102, Contact Rick Voight(+33-1-5534-2234) Circuit #FRT372826

Amsterdam(config-if)#ip address 192.168.4.1 255.255.255.0

Amsterdam(config-if)#frame-relay interface-dlci 102

Amsterdam(config-if)#interface serial 0.103 point-to-point

Amsterdam(config-if)#description PVC to Berlin, DLCI 103, Contact P Wills(+49- 61 03 / 7 65 72 00) Circuit #DTK465866

Amsterdam(config-if)#ip address 192.168.5.1 255.255.255.0

Amsterdam(config-if)#frame-relay interface-dlci 103
```

Task 4: Create Subinterfaces on the Paris Router

To configure the subinterfaces on the Paris router, use the following commands:

```
Paris(config-if)#interface Serial 0.201 point-to-point

Paris(config-if)#description PVC to Amsterdam, DLCI 201, Contact Peter Muller (+31 20 623 32 67) Circuit #KPN465555

Paris(config-if)#ip address 192.168.4.2 255.255.255.0

Paris(config-if)#frame-relay interface-dlci 201

Paris(config-if)#interface Serial 0.203 point-to-point

Paris(config-if)#description PVC to Berlin, DLCI 203, Contact Peter Willis (+49- 61 03 / 7 66 72 00) Circuit #DTK465866

Paris(config-if)#ip address 192.168.6.1 255.255.255.0

Paris(config-if)#frame-relay interface-dlci 203
```

Task 5: Create Subinterfaces on the Berlin Router

To configure the subinterfaces on the Berlin router, use the following commands:

```
Berlin(config-if)#interface Serial 0.301 point-to-point

Berlin(config-if)#description PVC to Amsterdam, DLCI 301, Contact Peter Muller (+31 20 623 32 67) Circuit #KPN465555

Berlin(config-if)#ip address 192.168.5.2 255.255.255.0

Berlin(config-if)#frame-relay interface-dlci 301

Berlin(config-if)#interface Serial 0.302 point-to-point

Berlin(config-if)#description PVC to Paris, DLCI 302, Contact Rick Voight (+33-1-5534-2234) Circuit #FRT372826

Berlin(config-if)#ip address 192.168.6.2 255.255.255.0

Berlin(config-if)#frame-relay interface-dlci 302
```

Task 6: Configure IGRP Routing

To configure the routing protocol IGRP 100, use the following configuration:

```
Amsterdam(config)#router igrp 100

Amsterdam(config-router)#network 192.168.1.0
```

```
Amsterdam(config-router)#network 192.168.4.0
Amsterdam(config-router)#network 192.168.5.0
```

```
Paris(config)#router igrp 100
Paris(config-router)#network 192.168.2.0
Paris(config-router)#network 192.168.4.0
Paris(config-router)#network 192.168.6.0
```

```
Berlin(config)#router igrp 100
Berlin(config-router)#network 192.168.3.0
Berlin(config-router)#network 192.168.5.0
Berlin(config-router)#network 192.168.6.0
```

Task 7: Verify the Frame Relay PVC

On the Amsterdam router, issue the command **show frame-relay pvc**:

```
Amsterdam#show frame-relay pvc
```

How many active local PVCs exist? _____

What is the interface value? _____

What is the PVC status? _____

Which DLCI number is inactive? _____

From this, you can see that three DLCIs are defined on this Frame Relay circuit, and only two of them are in use. This is the way the Adtran 550 emulator has been configured. It is useful output because it shows what you would see if a DLCI were defined on the Frame Relay switch but not configured on the router. The other DLCIs, 102 and 103, are active and are associated with their respective subinterfaces. It also shows that some packets have passed across the PVC.

Task 8: Show the Frame Relay Maps

Look at the Frame Relay maps by entering the command **show frame-relay map** at the privileged EXEC mode prompt:

```
Amsterdam#show frame-relay map
```

What is the status of the links? _____

What type are the DLCIs defined as? _____

Are the DLCIs the same on the Paris router? _____

Task 9: Show the LMIs

Look at the LMI statistics by using the **show frame-relay lmi** command:

```
Amsterdam#show frame-relay lmi
```

Which fields have nonzero counter values?

_____

What is the LMI type? _____

Task 10: Check the Routing Protocol

Step 1.   Use the **show ip route** command to verify that the PVCs are up and active:

Amsterdam#**show ip route**

Is the routing protocol working? _____

Step 2.   If not, troubleshoot the router configurations.

List the IGRP routes.

_____

_____

_____

_____

Task 11: Verify Connectivity

Step 1.   Ping the Fast Ethernet interfaces.

Did the pings succeed? _____

Step 2.   If not, troubleshoot the router configurations and repeat this task.

After you complete the previous tasks, log off (by entering **exit**) and turn the router off. Then, remove and store the cables and adapter.

Challenge Lab 5-4: Four-Interface Frame Relay Switch

This lab teaches you how to make a router into a four-interface Frame Relay switch. It is intended for use if an Adtran is unavailable. It lets you convert a router into a Frame Relay switch. You must have a WIC2T inserted in both WIC slots on the router. You can complete this lab using a 1721, 1760, or 2600 router that has two serial WICs available. Figure 5-4 presents the topology for this lab.

Figure 5-4   Network Topology for Lab 5-4

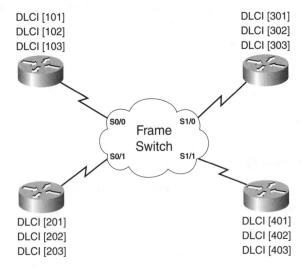

DLCI [101]
DLCI [102]
DLCI [103]

DLCI [301]
DLCI [302]
DLCI [303]

S0/0   S1/0
Frame Switch
S0/1   S1/1

DLCI [201]
DLCI [202]
DLCI [203]

DLCI [401]
DLCI [402]
DLCI [403]

Task 1

Erase the NVRAM and restart the router.

Task 2

Rename the router Frame_Switch:

```
Router(config)#Frame_Switch
```

Task 3

Enable Frame Relay switching on the router using the following command:

```
Frame_Switch (config)#frame-relay switching
```

This command enables you to create PVCs on the router interfaces. You must do this before configuring any interfaces.

Task 4

For the router to act as a Frame Relay switch, configure the following command on each interface:

```
Frame_Switch (config-if)#frame-relay interface-type dce
```

Task 5

Configure each router interface to use the IETF encapsulation type:

```
Frame_Switch (config-if)#encapsulation frame-relay ietf
```

Task 6

Configure Frame Relay PVC static routes on each interface. Following is a list of how each PVC should be mapped on the appropriate interfaces:

- Interface Serial 0/0:

  - DLCI 101 to DLCI 201 on interface Serial 0/1

  - DLCI 102 to DLCI 301 on interface Serial 1/0

  - DLCI 103 to DLCI 401 on interface Serial 1/1

- Interface Serial 0/1:

  - DLCI 201 to DLCI 101 on interface Serial 0/0

  - DLCI 202 to DLCI 302 on interface Serial 1/0

  - DLCI 203 to DLCI 402 on interface Serial 1/1

- Interface Serial 1/0:

  - DLCI 301 to DLCI 102 on interface Serial 0/0

  - DLCI 302 to DLCI 202 on interface Serial 1/0

  - DLCI 303 to DLCI 403 on interface Serial 1/1

- Interface Serial 1/1:

  - DLCI 401 to DLCI 103 on interface Serial 0/0

  - DLCI 402 to DLCI 203 on interface Serial 1/0

  - DLCI 403 to DLCI 303 on interface Serial 1/1

Task 7

Proceed to Challenge Lab 5-5, "Frame Relay Switch Challenge Lab 1."

Challenge Lab 5-5: Frame Relay Switch Challenge Lab 1

As the network administrator, you are required to set up a network using Frame Relay maps that will allow multiple Open Shortest Path First (OSPF) areas to communicate over a secure path through the Frame Relay cloud. You also need to set up the internal network addressing using virtual-length subnet masks (VLSMs) and classless interdomain routing (CIDR). You need a strong grasp of Dynamic Host Control Protocol (DHCP) and Network Address Translation (NAT) to complete this lab. Figure 5-5 shows the network topology for this lab using a Frame Relay switch, and Figure 5-6 shows the same topology using an Adtran.

Figure 5-5   Challenge Lab Diagram Using a Frame Relay Switch

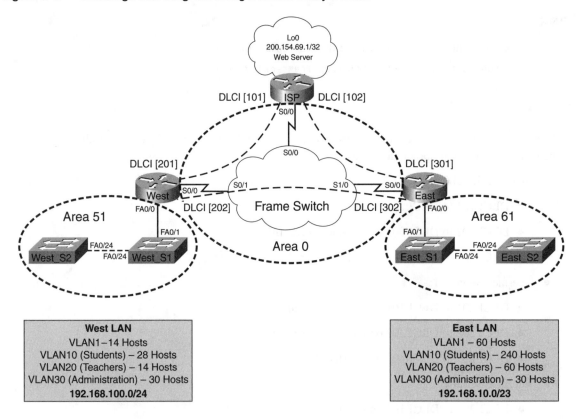

Figure 5-6   Challenge Lab Diagram Using an Adtran

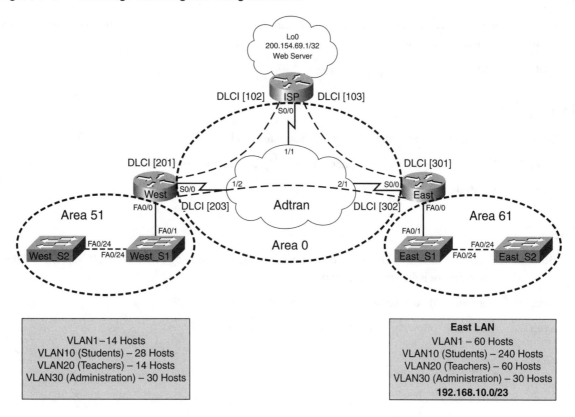

Table 5-4   Lab Equipment Configuration

Router Name	Serial Interface Address	Interface Type	Loopback 0 Address	DLCI Numbers	Enable Secret Password
ISP	64.53.18.1 /29	DTE	200.154.69.1/32	101, 102	cisco
East	64.53.18.2 /29	DTE	—	301, 302	cisco
West	64.53.18.3 /29	DTE	—	201, 202	cisco

Note:

This lab gives you the option of using a Frame Relay switch as the cloud or an Adtran if one is available. You can complete this lab exercise using any 1721, 1760, or 2600 series routers. The Frame Relay switch can be configured using Lab 5-4 and should follow the diagram in Figure 5-5 for the correct DLCI numbers. If an Adtran is available, follow the diagram in Figure 5-6 for the correct DLCI numbers.

Objectives

- Configure Frame Relay using a router as the Frame Switch.

- Multiple area OSPF with authentication.

- DHCP.

- NAT and PAT.

- VLANs and inter-VLAN routing.

Task 1

Cable and configure the equipment according to Figure 5-5 or 5-6, depending on whether you are using a Frame Relay switch or an Adtran.

Instructor's initials _____

Task 2

Step 1.   Configure Frame Relay using the appropriate DLCIs.

Step 2.   Ping each neighbor's serial interface to verify correct configuration.

Instructor's initials _____

Task 3

Step 1.   Configure East_Switch1 and West_Switch1 as VLAN Trunking Protocol (VTP) servers and the remaining switches as VTP clients.

Step 2.   Configure all switches as part of the **cisco** VTP domain.

Step 3.   Create the following VLANs on both server switches as follows:

- VLAN 1
- VLAN 10: Students
- VLAN 20: Teachers
- VLAN 30: Administrators

Step 4.   Assign the VLANs to the appropriate ports:

- VLAN 1: All unassigned ports
- VLAN 10: Ports 6–10 (ports 3–6 if you're using a 12-port switch)
- VLAN 20: Ports 11–15 (ports 7–9 if you're using a 12-port switch)
- VLAN 30: Ports 16–20 (ports 10–11 if you're using a 12-port switch)

Step 5.   Configure inter-VLAN routing using IEEE 802.1q encapsulation and the appropriate addressing scheme according to the diagram.

Instructor's initials _____

Task 4

Step 1.   Configure OSPF on each router using process ID 1.

Step 2.   With multiple areas inside the OSPF environment, be sure to use the appropriate wildcard mask and area ID.

Step 3.   The following commands must be configured on each OSPF router for Frame Relay to function across the Frame Switch. (Use Step 3 only when using a router as a Frame Relay switch.)

```
ISP(config)#router ospf 1
ISP(config-router)#neighbor 64.53.18.2 priority 1
ISP(config-router)#neighbor 64.53.18.3 priority 1
```

Step 4.   Verify functionality using the **show ip route** command.

Do not configure authentication yet!

Instructor's initials _____

Task 5

Step 1.   Configure DHCP on the East and West routers based on VLAN subnet information.

Step 2.   Exclude the first three addresses from each pool.

Instructor's initials _____

Task 6

Step 1.   Configure NAT on the East and West routers.

Step 2.   East router will use 24.83.68.0/25 for its NAT pool:

- Create a dynamic NAT pool for VLAN 1.
- All users from VLAN 10 will access the outside world using one IP address.
- All users from VLAN 20 will access the outside world using one IP address.
- Create a dynamic NAT pool for VLAN 30.

Step 3.   West router will use 161.73.29.0/26 for its NAT pool:

- Create a dynamic NAT pool for VLAN 1.
- Create a dynamic NAT pool for VLAN 10.
- Create a dynamic NAT pool for VLAN 20.
- All users from VLAN 30 will access the outside world using one IP address.

Instructor's initials _____

Task 7

Step 1.   Configure OSPF authentication on each router.

Step 2.   Configure the OSPF authentication key as **fred**.

You have the choice of using plain text or encrypted options for authentication.

Instructor's initials _____

Task 8

Configure the ISP router as a web server.

Instructor's initials _____

Task 9

Verify configuration using the appropriate commands. Hosts from each LAN should be able to open a browser and connect to the ISP web server.

Instructor's initials _____

Challenge Lab 5-6: Frame-Relay Challenge Lab 2

You are the network administrator of an international organization that has multiple sites around the world. Your task is to set up Frame Relay across the London, China, and Ireland routers. Enhanced Interior Gateway Routing Protocol (EIGRP) should be used to communicate between them. The Ireland and Scotland routers will use ISDN with static routes. In addition, you must set up the internal network off the Scotland router using VLSM, DHCP, and NAT. Figure 5-7 shows the network topology for this lab, and Table 5-5 lists the router interface details.

Figure 5-7   Network Topology for Challenge Lab 5-6

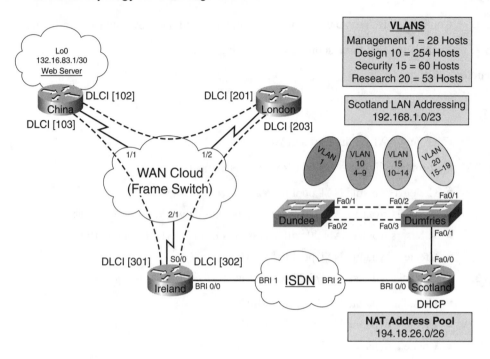

Table 5-5   Lab Equipment Configuration

Router Name	Serial Interface Address	Loopback 0 Address	Loopback 1 Address	Enable Secret
China	200.200.200.3/30	132.16.83.1/30	—	cisco
London	200.200.200.1/30	24.72.48.1/30	69.118.96.1/30	cisco
Ireland	200.200.200.2/30	—	—	cisco
Scotland	—	116.232.192.1/30	137.213.181.1/30	cisco

Note:

This lab can be done using any 1721, 1760, and 2600 series routers.

Objectives

- Configure Frame Relay.

- Configure ISDN using dialer profiles and interfaces.

- Use EIGRP as the routing protocol.

- Configure DHCP, NAT, and PAT.

- Configure VLANs and inter-VLAN routing.

Task 1

Cable and configure the equipment according to the diagram in Figure 5-7.

Instructor's initials _____

Task 2

Step 1.   Configure Frame Relay using the appropriate DLCIs.

Step 2.   Ping each neighbor's serial interface to verify correct configuration.

Instructor's initials _____

Task 3

Step 1.   Configure the Dumfries and Dundee switches with an available IP address from VLAN 1.

Step 2.   Configure the Dumfries switch as a VTP server and the Dundee switch as a VTP client.

Step 3.   Configure all switches as part of the cisco VTP domain.

Step 4.   Create the following VLANs:

- VLAN 1: Management
- VLAN 10: Design
- VLAN 15: Security
- VLAN 20: Research

Step 5.   Assign the VLANs to the appropriate ports:

- VLAN 1: All unassigned ports
- VLAN 10: Ports 4–9
- VLAN 15: Ports 10–14
- VLAN 20: Ports 15–19

Step 6.   Configure inter-VLAN routing using IEEE 802.1q encapsulation and the appropriate addressing scheme according to the diagram in Figure 5-7.

Instructor's initials _____

Task 4

Step 1.   Configure EIGRP on the London, China, and Ireland routers using AS100.

Step 2.   Create a default route on the Scotland router.

Step 3.   Create static routes on the Ireland router to the LAN addresses on the Scotland router, and point them to the dialer interface address of the Scotland router.

Step 4.   Propagate static routes inside the EIGRP domain.

Step 5.   Create a default route on the Scotland router, and point it to the dialer interface address of the Ireland router.

Step 6.   Verify functionality using the **show ip route** command on all routers.

Instructor's initials _____

Task 5

Step 1.   Configure ISDN on the Scotland and Ireland routers.

Step 2.   Use the appropriate SPIDs on the ISDN BRI interfaces.

Step 3.   Configure CHAP as the authentication protocol using **cisco** as the password.

Step 4.   Use the ISDN switch type basic-ni.

Step 5.   Allow ISDN to load-balance across both B channels.

Step 6.   Create dialer profiles.

Step 7.   Create dialer interfaces using the following addresses:

- Ireland: 193.15.63.1 255.255.255.252
- Scotland: 193.15.63.2 255.255.255.252

Step 8.   Allow all IP traffic to turn the ISDN line on.

Step 9.   Do not advertise either address in EIGRP. This will cause the interface to flap uncontrollably.

Instructor's initials _____

Task 6

Step 1.   Configure DHCP on the Scotland router.

Step 2.   Exclude the first three addresses from each pool.

Instructor's initials _____

Task 7

Step 1.   Configure NAT on the Scotland router.

Step 2.   Use the 194.18.26.0 /26 address for its NAT pool:

- Create a dynamic NAT pool for VLAN 1.
- All users from VLAN 10 will access the outside world using one IP address.
- Prevent VLAN 15 from accessing the outside world so that a NAT pool is not required.
- All users from VLAN 20 will access the outside world using one IP address.

Instructor's initials _____

Task 8

Configure the China router as an HTTP server.

Instructor's initials _____

Task 9

Verify configuration using the appropriate commands. DHCP-enabled hosts should receive a different address.

Instructor's initials _____

CHAPTER 6

Introduction to Network Administration

The Study Guide portion of this chapter uses a combination of multiple-choice and open-ended question exercises to test your knowledge of the theory of network administration.

This chapter contains no lab exercises.

Study Guide

Workstations and Servers

Workstations are regular computers that run multiple applications (word processing, spreadsheets, and so on) and allow multiple users to access information from a single location. They can run using one of several different platforms such as Windows, UNIX/Linux, or even Macintosh.

One specific type of workstation is a diskless workstation. A diskless workstation contains no drives for storage, making it unable to upload or download anything in the network. This aspect makes a diskless workstation ideal for networks that have security as a top priority. Laptops can serve as a mobile workstation if they are connected to the network (for example, wireless). Servers are workstations with different software and much more hardware, including memory and processing speed. This is because they must be operational all the time and capable of handling several simultaneous requests. Both servers and workstations have network operating systems that allow access to network resources and functions. Windows NT by Microsoft was the first network operating system designed to operate on large-scale networks with workgroup servers. Windows 2000 was then released as an "all-in-one" network operating system for large and small networks and single standalone computers. It also allows plug-and-play devices. Another version of a network operating system is UNIX, including variations such as Linux, which is an open-source programming code.

Concept Questions

1. Why is a diskless workstation preferred in a high-security situation as opposed to a regular workstation or a laptop?

_____

_____

_____

2. Compare and contrast Windows and UNIX platforms as network operating systems.

_____

_____

_____

_____

_____

_____

Network Management

Managing a network involves an array of tasks to keep the network operational, including the ability to grow or scale your network, routing and rerouting traffic, managing security, dealing with costs and budgets, and much more. Standards have been created for network management by the International Organization for Standardization (ISO). These standards are also encompassed within Simple Network Management Protocol (SNMP) and Common Management Information Protocol (CMIP), which both allow management of different platforms. SNMP is the most popular protocol used for managing corporate, connected networks. The four parts that allow SNMP to operate are a network management agent, station, information base, and protocol. The management station and agent work together to monitor occurrences such as the status of interfaces, virtual circuits, sent and received broadcast messages, and so on. Management Information Bases (MIBs) are used as banks of information about a device. Most MIBs are vendor-specific to help manage that particular device in the way it functions. Management agents are embedded within the software of network devices to send clear-text messages, or community strings, to the management station. A rule of thumb in SNMP is to collect the least amount of information over a widespread interval. The *string* acts as the message's password, and **ro** (read-only) and **rw** (read-write) tell whether the management station can make changes to the MIB.

Remote Monitoring (RMON) is a MIB that allows for remote monitoring of networks. It divides the task of monitoring into nine groups of aspects that it oversees: Statistics, History, Alarm, Host, HostTopN, Traffic Matrix, Filter, Packet Capture, and Event. Syslog is a utility used within Cisco devices to report errors. Syslog tags every error with a number, ranging from 0 to 7, that indicates the error's level of severity. If the syslog report has a 0 attached to it, the severity is great, whereas 7 indicates a minor severity. The level numbers are equivalent to the following (in order from 0 to 7): emergencies, alerts, critical, errors, warnings, notifications, informational, and debugging. The default severity level for all Cisco IOS syslog reports is 6. To enable syslog on a Cisco device, enter the command **logging on** in global configuration mode, which sends the logs to every destination that can read them. If there is a specific device to which the logs are to be sent, use the command **logging** [*ip address* | *hostname*].

Concept Questions

1. Management agents are embedded in the software of all network devices to report back to the management station. What are some of the things that the management agents keep track of and report to the management station?

_____

_____

_____

2. Explain how SNMP can be used in conjunction with software or other devices to enhance network monitoring.

_____

_____

_____

_____

Chapter Review Questions

For multiple-choice questions 1 through 20, circle the correct answers. Some questions have more than one answer.

1. What are the operating systems that a client workstation may operate on? (Select three)

    A. Sun Microsystems

    B. Windows

    C. Solaris

    D. UNIX

    E. Macintosh

2. What features of a diskless workstation provide security? (Select two)

    A. It contains no drives.

    B. It is used only for storage.

    C. It is unable to download or upload files.

    D. It is physically isolated from the rest of the network.

    E. All information is stored on an external hard drive.

3. There are workstations that perform low- and high-end tasks. What are some of the tasks that a high-end workstation may perform? (Select three)

    A. Word processing

    B. Graphic design

    C. Circuit design

    D. Spreadsheets

    E. Weather data analysis

4. Servers provide a variety of services on request from devices within the network. What are some of the services provided? (Select three)

    A. DHCP requests

    B. FTP file transfers

    C. Equipment management

    D. Print jobs

    E. Doubles as a backup workstation

5. Why are servers equipped with much more memory and processing power than a regular workstation? (Select two)

    A. They must be able to handle simultaneous requests from multiple workstations.

    B. They serve as a backup to every workstation in case one of them malfunctions.

    C. Servers are used for heavy data analysis and computer graphics animation.

    D. They function as storage facilities for network devices.

    E. Workstations are actually equipped with more hardware.

6. Which network operating system was released to operate on large and small-scale networks and remote computers?

    A. UNIX

    B. Windows 2000

    C. Windows NT

    D. Red Hat Linux

    E. Mac OS X

7. What protocols are used to help manage computer networks? (Select two)

    A. CMIP

    B. SMTP

    C. CMNP

    D. SNMP

    E. ISO Network Management Protocol

8. Which commands send all syslog entries to a specific location? (Select two)

    A. Router(config)#**logging** *ip address*

    B. Router(config-if)#**logging** *hostname*

    C. Router(config-if)#**logging** *ip address*

    D. Router(config)#**logging** *hostname*

    E. Router(config)#**logging** *syslog ip address*

9. What service does a Domain Name System (DNS) provide to a PC when accessing a website?

    A. It routes your request to the correct website.

    B. It provides the IP address for the website.

    C. It converts the website name into an IP address and then redirects your request to the website.

    D. It tells your router which path to take to get to the website.

10. Which devices in an SNMP-managed network communicate with one another and are responsible for reporting network errors?

    A. Management agent and protocol

    B. Management agent and information base

    C. Management station and agent

    D. Management protocol and information base

    E. Management station and information base

11. What are some of the things that a management agent can monitor about a particular device? (Select three)

    A. Status of virtual circuits

    B. Whether the device is powered on

    C. The size and number of packets that travel through the device

    D. If anyone is in a Telnet session in the network

    E. The states of the device's interfaces

12. What type of messages are sent to the remote management station from the management agents in the network?

    A. UDP error messages

    B. MD5 encrypted updates

    C. TCP synchronous messages

    D. TCP acknowledgments

    E. ICMP packets

13. A network management station (NMS) obtains information on the operation of the network from a MIB. What message types does the MIB send back to the NMS? (Select three)

    A. Bulk

    B. Get

    C. Set

    D. Log

    E. Trap

14. When SNMPv2c was introduced, what two additional functions were added?

A. GetNextRequest

B. SetRequest

C. GetBulkRequest

D. 64-bit counters

E. GetRequestBulk

15. What is true about the command **snmp-server community** *string* **rw**?

A. The management station can obtain only MIB objects.

B. The management station can create a copy of the information base.

C. The management station and other local devices may modify the MIB.

D. The management station can retrieve and change MIB items.

E. The management station cannot do anything at all.

16. The syslog utility in Cisco is used to mark errors with a severity level number ranging from 0 to 7. What is the default severity level?

A. Notifications

B. Informational

C. Debugging

D. Emergencies

E. Alerts

17. What command tells the device where to send all SNMP entries?

A. Router(config)#**snmp-server manage** *text*

B. Router(config-if)#**snmp-server agent** *text*

C. Router(config)#**snmp-server location** *text*

D. Router(config)#**snmp-server agent** *text*

E. Router(config-if)#**snmp-server manage** *text*

18. What is the purpose of the SNMP **community** string? (Select two)

A. It is the name of the router connecting to the SNMP server.

B. It acts like a password.

C. It is encrypted.

D. It is in plain text.

19. What are the four parts of the ISO model for network management?

A. Organization

B. Information

C. Fault

D. Configuration

E. Communication

F. Performance

G. Functional

20. What feature of the MAC OS X is considered a cross between Microsoft Windows XP and Linux X Window System GUI?

- **A.** Apple
- **B.** Aqua
- **C.** Darwin
- **D.** AppleTalk

Lab Exercises

This chapter contains no lab exercises.

Troubleshooting Questions and Lab Exercise

Troubleshooting Questions

1. Which of the following display when you use the command **show controller serial 0**? (Select all that apply)

   A. Clock rate

   B. Bandwidth

   C. Cable type

   D. DTE or DCE

   E. Line up, protocol up

2. When troubleshooting OSPF, which of the following would cause configuration issues? (Select all that apply)

   A. Incorrect timers

   B. Misconfigured areas

   C. Authentication seen in plain text

   D. Incorrect address and subnet mask

   E. No DR and BDR

3. Which command displays the WAN encapsulation currently being used?

   A. **show encapsulation**

   B. **show ip route**

   C. **show interface serial 0**

   D. **show ip interface serial 0**

4. Which of the following display when you use the **show ip route** command? (Select all that apply)

   A. Metric

   B. Routing protocol

   C. Line up, protocol down

   D. Connected networks

   E. Learned networks

   F. Name of router advertising learned routes

   G. Number of routers in network

5. What commands are necessary when you completely erase a switch's configurations? (Select all that apply)

   A. **erase startup-config**

   B. **delete flash**

   C. **reboot**

   D. **delete flash:vlan.dat**

   E. **reload**

   F. **erase running-config**

6. Which of the following would cause a Frame Relay connection to fail when using map statements? (Select all that apply)

    A. Misconfigured DLCI

    B. Inverse ARP disabled

    C. Broadcast statement missing

    D. Misconfigured routing protocol

    E. Misconfigured map statements

7. Which of the following must be done for a successful PAT configuration? (Select all that apply)

    A. Create an ACL

    B. Create a NAT pool

    C. Static keyword

    D. Overload keyword

    E. Apply ACL to NAT pool

    F. Sufficient number of addresses in NAT pool

8. Which command produces the following output?

```
*Mar  1 00:40:52.202: ISDN BR1/0 Q921: User RX <- RRp sapi=0 tei=64 nr=21
*Mar  1 00:40:52.202: ISDN BR1/0 Q921: User TX -> RRf sapi=0 tei=64 nr=14
*Mar  1 00:40:52.467: %ISDN-6-DISCONNECT: Interface BRI1/0:1  disconnected from
5552000 Scotland, call lasted 430 seconds
*Mar  1 00:40:52.471: ISDN BR1/0 Q921: User TX -> INFO sapi=0 tei=64, ns=21 nr=1
4
*Mar  1 00:40:52.499: ISDN BR1/0 Q921: User RX <- RR sapi=0 tei=64 nr=22
*Mar  1 00:40:52.511: ISDN BR1/0 Q921: User RX <- INFO sapi=0 tei=64, ns=14 nr=2
2
*Mar  1 00:40:52.515: ISDN BR1/0 Q921: User TX -> RR sapi=0 tei=64 nr=15
*Mar  1 00:40:52.515: %LINK-3-UPDOWN: Interface BRI1/0:1, changed state to down
*Mar  1 00:40:52.519: %DIALER-6-UNBIND: Interface BR1/0:1 unbound from profile D
```

    A. debug isdn

    B. debug isdn status

    C. debug q931

    D. debug q921

9. What command displays the number of ISDN lines that were established?

    A. show interface serial 0

    B. show encapsulation ppp

    C. show isdn active

    D. show dialer

10. Which command propagates a default route when you use OSPF?

    A. redistribute static

    B. Nothing (because it's automatic)

    C. default information-originate

    D. redistribute default

11. Which of the following causes an EIGRP route to be put in the "Stuck in active" state?

    A. Misconfigured area

    B. Misconfigured timers

    C. Wrong autonomous system number

    D. No response from a query

    E. DUAL not working properly

12. What must be done for a router to become the DR in an OSPF environment?

    A. Assign it the highest-priority number.

    B. Assign it the highest loopback address.

    C. Assign it the highest configured IP address on one of its interfaces.

    D. Put at least one interface in area 0.

13. What should be added to the end of a static route to make sure it is used only when the primary routing protocol goes down?

    A. High metric

    B. Low metric

    C. Higher administrative distance than the routing protocol

    D. Lower administrative distance than the routing protocol

    E. Nothing

14. What command displays real-time events as they occur on a router?

    A. **show**

    B. **debug**

    C. **show run**

    D. **show events**

15. You are running RIPv2 in your network and have a destination that is reachable by some locations but not by all. Which of the following causes this problem to occur?

    A. There are more than 15 routers in your network.

    B. The **network** statement was not properly configured.

    C. The network was not being advertised.

    D. The network is down.

16. Which command displays the DHCP addresses currently in use?

    A. **show ip dhcp**

    B. **show ip dhcp addresses**

    C. **show ip dhcp binding**

    D. **show ip dhcp statistics**

17. Which of the following causes the following to occur: "Serial 0 is up, line protocol is down"? (Select all that apply)

    A. Clock rate not detected

    B. Administratively down

    C. No keepalives

    D. Wrong clock rate

18. Which command produces the following output?

```
BRI1/0 - dialer type = ISDN

Dial String      Successes   Failures    Last DNIS   Last status
0 incoming call(s) have been screened.
0 incoming call(s) rejected for callback.

BRI1/0:1 - dialer type = ISDN
Idle timer (120 secs), Fast idle timer (20 secs)
Wait for carrier (30 secs), Re-enable (15 secs)
Dialer state is idle

BRI1/0:2 - dialer type = ISDN
Idle timer (120 secs), Fast idle timer (20 secs)
Wait for carrier (30 secs), Re-enable (15 secs)
Dialer state is idle

Di0 - dialer type = DIALER PROFILE
Idle timer (120 secs), Fast idle timer (20 secs)
Wait for carrier (30 secs), Re-enable (15 secs)
Dialer state is idle
Number of active calls = 0
```

   A. show isdn status

   B. show dialer

   C. show isdn dialer

   D. show q921

19. Which routing protocols are suitable for VLSM and CIDR? (Select all that apply)

   A. RIP

   B. RIPv2

   C. OSPF

   D. EIGRP

   E. IGRP

   F. Static routes

   G. IS-IS

20. You just configured a switch and noticed that it is not propagating the VLAN information to the other switches on your network. What would cause this to happen? (Select all that apply)

   A. The switch is in the wrong domain.

   B. Misconfigured VLAN numbers

   C. The switch is in server mode.

   D. The switch is in transparent mode.

   E. The switch is in client mode.

21. You configured NAT on a router that is using inter-VLAN routing. You put the **ip nat inside** command on the physical interface and the **ip nat outside** command on the outside interface, but nothing is being translated. You checked your configurations, and everything was done correctly. What could be the problem?

   A. There are too many hosts with not enough addresses.

   B. The **ip nat inside** command should be put on the subinterfaces.

   C. The **ip nat inside** command should be put on the outside interface.

   D. PAT is being used.

22. You work for an ISP. A customer needs an IP address for 4519 hosts. You decide to summarize a group of Class C addresses because a Class B would waste a large number of addresses. How many Class C addresses need to be summarized?

   A. 1

   B. 10

   C. 15

   D. 18

23. Which command produces the following?

```
Pro Inside global       Inside local        Outside local       Outside global
--- 194.18.26.1         192.168.100.99      ---                 ---
--- 194.18.26.2         192.168.100.98      ---                 ---
--- 194.18.26.15        192.168.100.66      ---                 ---
```

   A. **show ip dhcp binding**

   B. **show ip nat translations**

   C. **show nat translations**

   D. **show translations**

24. Which of the following does LCP negotiate when establishing a PPP connection?

   A. Q.931

   B. IPCP

   C. Multilink

   D. CHAP

   E. Callback

25. Which command would you use to terminate a vty session?

   A. **close**

   B. **disable**

   C. **disconnect**

   D. **suspend**

   E. **exit**

26. If you can dial across an ISDN connection but your session is dropped immediately upon connecting, what could be the cause? (Select two)

   A. Incorrect SPIDs

   B. LCP not connecting

   C. Username and passwords were not set.

   D. Wrong username and/or password

27. Which command produces the following output?

```
Codes: P - Passive, A - Active, U - Update, Q - Query, R - Reply,
       r - reply Status, s - sia Status


P 24.0.0.0/8, 1 successors, FD is 20640000
        via 200.200.200.1 (20640000/128256), Serial0/0
P 69.0.0.0/8, 1 successors, FD is 20640000
        via 200.200.200.1 (20640000/128256), Serial0/0
P 116.232.192.0/30, 1 successors, FD is 40512000
        via Rstatic (40512000/0)
P 132.16.0.0/16, 1 successors, FD is 20640000
        via 200.200.200.3 (20640000/128256), Serial0/0
P 200.200.200.0/24, 1 successors, FD is 20512000
        via Connected, Serial0/0
P 194.18.26.0/26, 1 successors, FD is 46226176
```

   A. show ip protocol

   B. show ip ospf database

   C. show ip eigrp topology

   D. show ip eigrp neighbors

28. Which command produces the following output?

```
IP address          Hardware address        Lease expiration        Type
192.168.100.3       0100.1422.3497.93       Mar 02 1993 12:14 AM    Automatic
192.168.100.66      0100.123f.49e5.20       Mar 02 1993 12:33 AM    Automatic
```

   A. show dhcp addresses

   B. show ip dhcp addresses

   C. show ip dhcp binding

   D. show ip nat translations

29. In an ISDN environment, what would be the result of advertising the dialer interface over a routing protocol?

   A. Routing protocols are corrupted.

   B. The dialer interface continuously flaps.

   C. The network will not be advertised in routing updates.

   D. Nothing; everything would work fine.

30. What is the purpose of the **frame-relay inverse-arp** command?

   A. To create dynamic maps

   B. To create an ARP table across a Frame Relay network

   C. To create static maps

   D. To reverse the inverse table of RARP

Lab A-1: WAN Troubleshooting

Figure A-1   Topology for Lab A-1

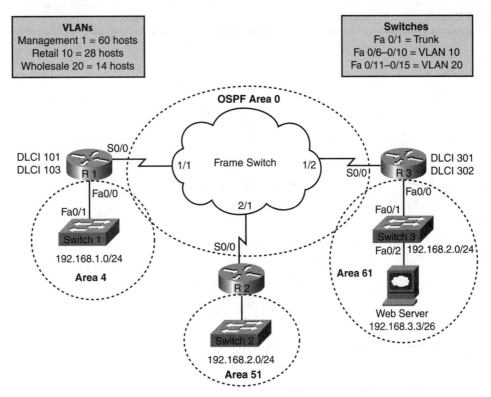

Complete the lab exercise by isolating and correcting the problems outlined in the scenario. This lab tests your ability to use a troubleshooting methodology and commands to isolate and correct network problems. When complete, all hosts should be able to telnet and ping to each device in the network. Make sure that the diagram is correctly cabled before proceeding.

Objectives

■ List problems found and document corrections that solve each issue.

■ Verify that the network has been restored and that no new problems were created from unnecessary changes.

Scenario

You are the "on-call" network administrator for the weekend, and so far nothing new has come up. You decide to enjoy the afternoon by catching a movie with your friends when you receive an urgent message "Please call the office immediately; nothing seems to be working, and the network is down." You call the office and find out that a disgruntled ex-employee sabotaged the network. You leave for the office immediately, to the dismay of your friends.

Back at the office, you find the following problems:

■ You are unable to get into the R1 router.

■ Routes from remote locations are not seen.

■ NAT is not functioning properly on Router 2 for the Wholesale department.

■ Hosts on the R3 LAN cannot access the network.

Troubleshooting Log

Fill in the problems and solutions for each network device in the following table.

Network Device	Problems	Solutions
R1		
Switch_1		
R2		
Switch_2		
R3:		
Switch_3		

Student name _____

Instructor's initials _____

Bugged Configs

```
R1#show running-config
Building configuration...

Current configuration : 2226 bytes
!
version 12.2
service timestamps debug datetime msec
service timestamps log datetime msec
no service password-encryption
!
hostname R1
!
enable secret 5 $1$Lt15$vAE/GOt4IUUmeXxn8ZZPR1
!
ip subnet-zero
ip dhcp excluded-address 192.168.1.1 192.168.1.2
ip dhcp excluded-address 192.168.1.65
```

```
!
ip dhcp pool Management
    network 192.168.1.0 255.255.255.192
    default-router 192.168.1.1
!
ip dhcp pool Retail
    network 192.168.1.64 255.255.255.224
    default-router 192.168.1.65


!
!
!
!
!
interface FastEthernet0/0
no shut
no ip address
speed auto
!
interface FastEthernet0/0.1
description Management VLAN
encapsulation dot1Q 1 native
ip address 192.168.1.1 255.255.255.192
ip nat inside
!
interface FastEthernet0/0.10
description Retail VLAN
encapsulation dot1Q 10
ip address 192.168.1.65 255.255.255.224
ip nat inside
!
interface FastEthernet0/0.20
description Wholesale VLAN

encapsulation dot1Q 20
ip address 192.168.1.97 255.255.255.240
ip nat inside
!
interface Serial0/0
no shut
description To WAN Cloud
ip address 10.10.10.1 255.255.255.248
ip nat outside
encapsulation frame-relay
ip ospf authentication-key cisco
```

```
ip ospf network point-to-point
no fair-queue
frame-relay map ip 10.10.10.2 101
frame-relay map ip 10.10.10.3 103
!
interface Serial0/1
no ip address
shutdown
!
interface BRI1/0
no ip address
shutdown
!

router ospf 1
log-adjacency-changes
area 0 authentication
network 10.10.10.1 0.0.0.0 area 0
network 192.168.1.1 0.0.0.0 area 4
network 192.168.1.65 0.0.0.0 area 4
network 192.168.1.97 0.0.0.0 area 4
!
ip nat pool Management 63.49.18.1 63.49.18.60 netmask 255.255.255.0
ip nat pool Retail 63.49.18.65 63.49.18.65 netmask 255.255.255.0
ip nat pool Wholesale 63.49.18.97 63.49.18.110 netmask 255.255.255.0
ip nat inside source list 1 pool Management
ip nat inside source list 2 pool Retail overload
ip nat inside source list 3 pool Wholesale
ip classless
ip route 181.16.57.0 255.255.255.0 10.10.10.2
ip route 200.169.54.0 255.255.255.0 10.10.10.3
no ip http server
!
!
access-list 1 permit 192.168.1.0 0.0.0.63
access-list 2 permit 192.168.1.64 0.0.0.31
access-list 3 permit 192.168.1.96 0.0.0.15

!
line con 0
logging synch
password class
login
line aux 0
line vty 0 4
```

```
password cisco
login
!
end
```

```
R2#show running-config
Building configuration...

Current configuration : 2260 bytes
!
version 12.2
service timestamps debug datetime msec
service timestamps log datetime msec
no service password-encryption
!
hostname R2
!
!
ip subnet-zero
ip dhcp excluded-address 192.168.2.1 192.168.2.2
ip dhcp excluded-address 192.168.2.65
ip dhcp excluded-address 192.168.2.97
!
ip dhcp pool Management
   network 192.168.2.0 255.255.255.192
   default-router 192.168.2.1
!
ip dhcp pool Retail
   network 192.168.2.64 255.255.255.224

   default-router 192.168.2.65
!
ip dhcp pool Wholesale
   network 192.168.2.96 255.255.255.240
   default-router 192.168.2.97
!
!
!
!
!
interface FastEthernet0/0
no shut
no ip address
speed auto
!
```

```
interface FastEthernet0/0.1
description Management
encapsulation dot1Q 1 native
ip address 192.168.2.1 255.255.255.192
ip nat inside
!
interface FastEthernet0/0.10
description Retail
encapsulation dot1Q 10

ip address 192.168.2.65 255.255.255.224
ip nat inside
!
interface FastEthernet0/0.20
description Wholesale
encapsulation dot1Q 20
ip address 192.168.2.97 255.255.255.240
ip nat inside
!
interface Serial0/0
no shut
description to WAN Cloud
ip address 10.10.10.2 255.255.255.248
ip nat outside
encapsulation frame-relay
ip ospf authentication-key cysco
ip ospf network point-to-multipoint
no fair-queue
frame-relay map ip 10.10.10.1 202 Broadcast
frame-relay map ip 10.10.10.3 203 Broadcast
!
interface Serial0/1
no ip address
shutdown

!
router ospf 1
log-adjacency-changes
area 0 authentication
network 10.10.10.2 0.0.0.0 area 0
network 192.168.2.1 0.0.0.0 area 51
network 192.168.2.65 0.0.0.0 area 51
network 192.168.2.97 0.0.0.0 area 51
!
```

```
ip nat pool Management 181.16.57.1 181.16.57.60 netmask 255.255.255.0
ip nat pool Retail 181.16.57.65 181.16.57.87 netmask 255.255.255.0
ip nat pool Wholesale 181.16.57.97 181.16.57.110 netmask 255.255.255.0
ip nat inside source list 1 pool Marketing
ip nat inside source list 2 pool Retail
ip nat inside source list 3 pool Wholesale
ip classless
ip route 63.49.18.0 255.255.255.0 10.10.10.1
ip route 200.169.54.0 255.255.255.0 10.10.10.3
no ip http server
!
!
access-list 1 permit 192.168.2.0 0.0.0.63
access-list 2 permit 192.168.2.64 0.0.0.31

!
line con 0
logging synch
password class
login
line aux 0
line vty 0 4
password cisco
login
!
end

R2#
```

```
R3#show running-config
Building configuration...

Current configuration : 2420 bytes
!
version 12.2
service timestamps debug datetime msec
service timestamps log datetime msec
no service password-encryption
!
hostname R3
!
!
ip subnet-zero
ip dhcp excluded-address 192.168.3.1 192.168.3.2
```

```
ip dhcp excluded-address 192.168.3.65
ip dhcp excluded-address 192.168.3.97
!
ip dhcp pool Management
    network 192.168.3.0 255.255.255.192
    default-router 192.168.3.1
!
ip dhcp pool Retail
    network 192.168.3.96 255.255.255.224


!
ip dhcp pool Wholesale
    network 192.168.3.96 255.255.255.240
    default-router 192.168.3.97
!
!
!
!
!
interface FastEthernet0/0
no shut
no ip address
speed auto
!
interface FastEthernet0/0.1
description Management VLAN
encapsulation dot1Q 1 native
ip address 192.168.3.1 255.255.255.192
ip nat inside
!
interface FastEthernet0/0.10
description Retail VLAN
encapsulation dot1Q 10
ip address 192.168.3.65 255.255.255.224

ip nat inside
!
interface FastEthernet0/0.20
description Wholesale VLAN
encapsulation dot1Q 20
ip address 192.168.3.97 255.255.255.240
ip nat inside
!
interface Serial0/0
no shut
description To WAN cloud
```

```
ip address 10.10.10.3 255.255.255.240
ip nat outside
encapsulation frame-relay
ip ospf authentication-key cisco
ip ospf network point-to-multipoint
no fair-queue
frame-relay map ip 10.10.10.1 302 Broadcast
frame-relay map ip 10.10.10.2 301 Broadcast
!
interface Serial0/1
no ip address
shutdown
!
interface BRI1/0
no ip address
shutdown
!
router ospf 1
log-adjacency-changes
area 0 authentication
network 10.10.10.3 0.0.0.0 area 0
network 192.168.3.1 0.0.0.0 area 61
network 192.168.3.65 0.0.0.0 area 61
network 192.168.3.97 0.0.0.0 area 61
!
ip nat pool Management 200.169.54.4 200.169.54.60 netmask 255.255.255.0
ip nat pool Retail 200.169.54.65 200.169.54.87 netmask 255.255.255.0
ip nat pool Wholesale 200.169.54.97 200.169.54.97 netmask 255.255.255.0
ip nat inside source list 1 pool Management
ip nat inside source list 2 pool Retail
ip nat inside source list 3 pool Wholesale overload
ip nat inside source static 192.168.3.3 200.169.54.3
ip classless
ip route 63.49.18.0 255.255.255.0 10.10.10.1
ip route 181.16.57.0 255.255.255.0 10.10.10.2
no ip http server
!
!
access-list 1 permit 192.168.3.0 0.0.0.63
access-list 2 permit 192.168.3.64 0.0.0.31
access-list 3 permit 192.168.3.96 0.0.0.15
!
line con 0
password class
logging synchronous
login
```

```
line aux 0
line vty 0 4
password cisco
login
!
end


R3#
```

```
Switch1#show running-config
Building configuration...

Current configuration : 1443 bytes
!
version 12.1
no service pad
service timestamps debug uptime
service timestamps log uptime
no service password-encryption
!
hostname Switch1
!
VLAN 10
name Retail
VLAN 20
name Wholesale
exit
!
ip subnet-zero
!
!
spanning-tree mode pvst
no spanning-tree optimize bpdu transmission
spanning-tree extend system-id
!
!
!
!
interface FastEthernet0/1

switchport trunk native  2
switchport mode trunk
!
interface FastEthernet0/2
!
```

```
interface FastEthernet0/3
!
interface FastEthernet0/4
!
interface FastEthernet0/5
!
interface FastEthernet0/6
switchport access vlan 10
!
interface FastEthernet0/7
switchport access vlan 10
!
interface FastEthernet0/8
switchport access vlan 10
!
interface FastEthernet0/9
switchport access vlan 10
!

interface FastEthernet0/10
switchport access vlan 10
!
interface FastEthernet0/11
switchport access vlan 20
!
interface FastEthernet0/12
switchport access vlan 20
!
interface FastEthernet0/13
switchport access vlan 20
!
interface FastEthernet0/14
switchport access vlan 20
!
interface FastEthernet0/15
switchport access vlan 20
!
interface FastEthernet0/16
!
interface FastEthernet0/17
!
interface FastEthernet0/18

!
interface FastEthernet0/19
```

```
!
interface FastEthernet0/20
!
interface FastEthernet0/21
!
interface FastEthernet0/22
!
interface FastEthernet0/23
!
interface FastEthernet0/24
!
interface Vlan1
ip address 192.168.1.2 255.255.255.192
no ip route-cache
no shut
!
ip default-gateway 192.168.1.1
ip http server
!
line con 0
logging synch
line vty 0 4
password cisco
login
line vty 5 15
password cisco
login


!


end
```

```
Switch2#show running-config
Building configuration...

Current configuration : 1421 bytes
!
version 12.1
no service pad
service timestamps debug uptime
service timestamps log uptime
no service password-encryption
!
hostname Switch2
```

```
!
vlan 10
name Retail
vlan 20
name Wholesale
exit
!
ip subnet-zero
!
!
spanning-tree mode pvst
no spanning-tree optimize bpdu transmission
spanning-tree extend system-id
!
!
!
!
interface FastEthernet0/1

switchport mode trunk
shutdown
!
interface FastEthernet0/2
!
interface FastEthernet0/3
!
interface FastEthernet0/4
!
interface FastEthernet0/5
!
interface FastEthernet0/6
switchport access vlan 10
!
interface FastEthernet0/7
switchport access vlan 10
!
interface FastEthernet0/8
switchport access vlan 10
!
interface FastEthernet0/9
switchport access vlan 10
!

interface FastEthernet0/10
switchport access vlan 10
```

```
!
interface FastEthernet0/11
switchport access vlan 20
!
interface FastEthernet0/12
switchport access vlan 20
!
interface FastEthernet0/13
switchport access vlan 20
!
interface FastEthernet0/14
switchport access vlan 20
!
interface FastEthernet0/15
switchport access vlan 20
!
interface FastEthernet0/16
!
interface FastEthernet0/17
!
interface FastEthernet0/18

!
interface FastEthernet0/19
!
interface FastEthernet0/20
!
interface FastEthernet0/21
!
interface FastEthernet0/22
!
interface FastEthernet0/23
!
interface FastEthernet0/24
!
interface Vlan1
ip address 192.168.2.2 255.255.255.192
no ip route-cache
no shut
!
ip default-gateway 192.168.2.1
ip http server
```

```
!
line con 0
logging sync
line vty 5 15
!


end
```

```
Switch3#show running-config
Building configuration...

Current configuration : 1524 bytes
!
version 12.1
no service pad
service timestamps debug uptime
service timestamps log uptime
no service password-encryption
!
hostname Switch3
!
vlan 10
name Retail
vlan 20
name Wholesale
exit
!
ip subnet-zero
!
!
spanning-tree mode pvst
no spanning-tree optimize bpdu transmission
spanning-tree extend system-id
!
!
interface FastEthernet0/1
switchport mode trunk
no ip address

!
interface FastEthernet0/2
no ip address
!
interface FastEthernet0/3
no ip address
```

```
!
interface FastEthernet0/4
no ip address
!
interface FastEthernet0/5
no ip address
!
interface FastEthernet0/6
no ip address
!
interface FastEthernet0/7
no ip address
!
interface FastEthernet0/8
no ip address
!
interface FastEthernet0/9

no ip address
!
interface FastEthernet0/10
no ip address
!
interface FastEthernet0/11
no ip address
!
interface FastEthernet0/12
no ip address
!
interface FastEthernet0/13
no ip address
!
interface FastEthernet0/14
no ip address
!
interface FastEthernet0/15
no ip address
!
interface FastEthernet0/16
no ip address
```

```
!
interface FastEthernet0/17
no ip address
!
interface FastEthernet0/18
no ip address
!
interface FastEthernet0/19
no ip address
!
interface FastEthernet0/20
no ip address
!
interface FastEthernet0/21
no ip address
!
interface FastEthernet0/22
no ip address
!
interface FastEthernet0/23
no ip address
!
interface FastEthernet0/24

!
interface FastEthernet0/22
no ip address
!
interface FastEthernet0/23
no ip address
!
interface FastEthernet0/24
no ip address
!
interface Vlan1
ip address 192.168.3.2 255.255.255.192
no ip route-cache
no shut
!
ip default-gateway 192.168.3.1
ip http server
!
!
```

```
line con 0
logging sync
line vty 0 4
password cisco
login
line vty 5 15
password cisco
login
end
```

Adtran Configuration Lab

Objectives

- Manually configure an Adtran for ISDN, Frame Relay, and POTS.
- Verify configurations.

Task 1: Log in to Adtran

Step 1. Use a straight-through cable from the PC NIC to the Adtran Ethernet port.

Step 2. Configure the PC to IP address 10.0.0.2/24.

Step 3. Open the command prompt and enter the following command (see Figure B-1):

`C:\>telnet 10.0.0.1`

The default IP address for the Ethernet interface on the Adtran is 10.0.0.1.

This allows you to telnet into the Adtran.

Figure B-1   Telnet to Adtran

Step 4. Enter the default login password of **password** (see Figure B-2).

Figure B-2   Insert Default Password at Login Screen

Task 2: Set Up ISDN BRI Switch Emulation

Step 1.   Using the arrow keys, scroll down to Dial Plan on the left (see Figure B-3).

Figure B-3   Main Menu of the Adtran

Note

The mouse will not work in this mode.

Step 2.   Using the right-arrow key, select **User Term** (see Figure B-4).

Figure B-4   Select User Term

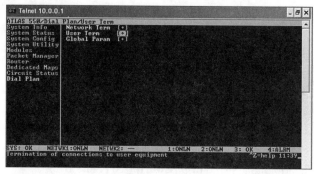

Step 3.   Configure the ISDN Slot info (see Figure B-5).

Press **Enter** to change the **Slot/Service** setting.

Slot 1: U-BRI-4

Figure B-5   Configure User Term

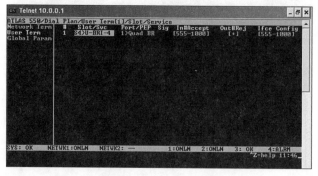

Step 4. Using the right arrow, change the **Port/Packet Endpoint (PEP)** setting as follows:

Port 1: QUAD BRI (see Figure B-5)

Step 5. Using the right arrow, scroll to the **In#Accept** value and press **Enter**.

Select **Accept Number** and press **Enter** (see Figure B-6).

Figure B-6   Configure Two Accept Numbers

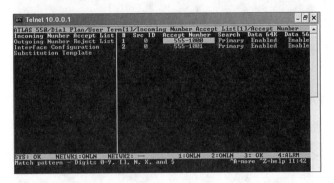

Step 6. Configure two numbers per slot (see Figure B-6).

1st Port number: 555-1000

2nd Port number: 555-1001

Note

To insert a new line, press the letter **I**.

To delete a line, press the letter **D**.

Return to the preceding screen.

Step 7. Select an interface under Slot/Svc and press **Enter** (see Figure B-7).

Figure B-7   Select an Interface

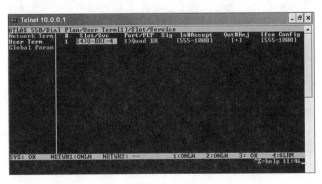

Step 8. Select **Interface Configuration** (see Figure B-8).

Select **SPID list** and press **Enter**.

Figure B-8   Select SPID List

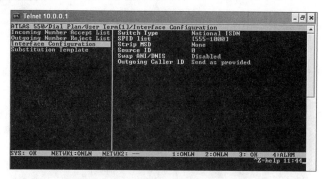

Step 9.   Configure the SPID list as shown for each port (see Figure B-9).

Figure B-9   Configure SPID List

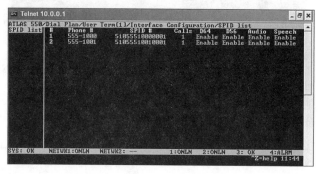

Step 10.   Repeat Steps 3 through 9 for all four ISDN ports.

When you have finished, the configuration should look like Figure B-10.

Figure B-10   Completed Configuration of ISDN Ports

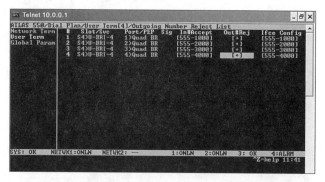

Note

When selecting port/PEP, each port must be a different number:

- Slot 1: 1>QUAD BR

- Slot 2: 2>QUAD BR

and so on.

Press the left-arrow key until you return to the main menu.

Task 3: Set Up Analog POTS Switch Emulation (from the Main Menu)

Step 1.   Scroll down to **Dial Plan** and press **Enter** (see Figure B-11).

Figure B-11   Select a Dial Plan

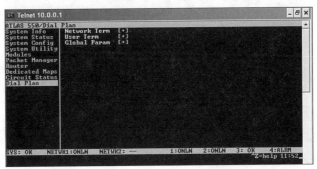

Step 2.   Select **User Term** (see Figure B-12) and press **Enter**.

Figure B-12   Select User Term

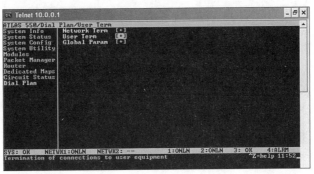

Step 3.   Configure a fifth line with the slot configured for FXS-8 (see Figure B-13).

Configure **Port/PEP** as FXS 3/1.

To insert a new line, press the letter **I**.

Figure B-13   Create and Configure a Fifth Line

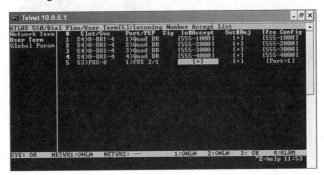

Step 4.   Select **In#Accept**.

Configure the **Accept Number** as shown (see Figure B-14).

Figure B-14   Configure the Accept Number

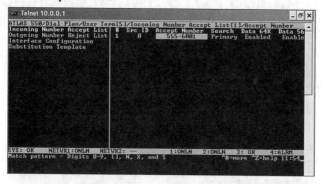

Task 4: Configuring Frame Relay (from the Main Menu)

Step 1.   Scroll down and select **Packet Manager** (see Figure B-15).

Select **Packet Endpoints** and press **Enter**.

Figure B-15   Select Packet Endpoints

Step 2.   Select **Config** and press **Enter** (see Figure B-16).

Figure B-16   Select Config

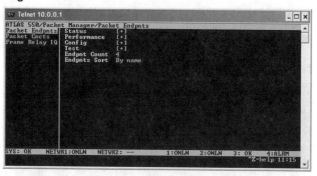

Step 3.   Configure endpoints as shown (see Figure B-17).

Name each endpoint.

Select **Frame Relay Protocol** for each.

Using the right-arrow key, move over to **Config** and press **Enter**.

Figure B-17   Configure Each Endpoint Name

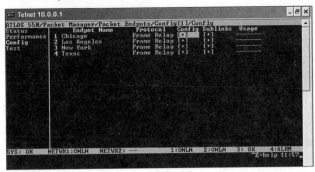

Note

To insert a new line, press the letter **I**.

To delete a line, press the letter **D**.

Return to the preceding screen.

Step 4.   Configure Signaling Role as **Network** (see Figure B-18).

Configure Signaling Type as **Annex D**.

Scroll down to **Sublinks** and press **Enter**.

Figure B-18   Configure Signaling Type

Step 5.   Configure as shown in Figures B-19, B-20, B-21, and B-22.

Name DLCIs and DLCI number for each sublink.

Figure B-19   Chicago Port

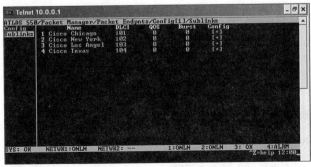

Figure B-20   Los Angeles Port

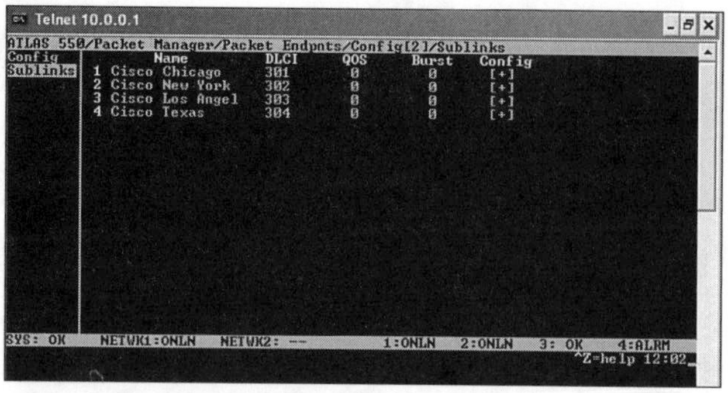

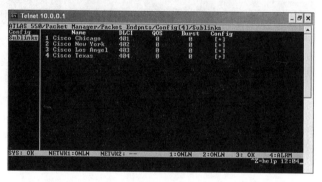

Figure B-21   New York Port

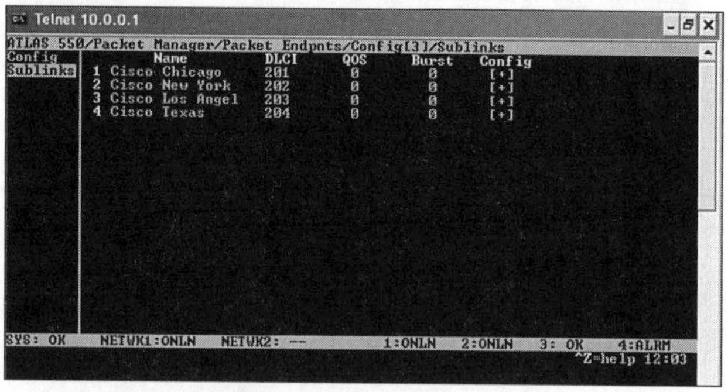

Figure B-22   Texas Port

Step 6.   Repeat Steps 4 and 5 for each Frame Relay port.

Note

To insert a new line, press the letter **I**.

To delete a line, press the letter **D**.

Return to the preceding screen.

Step 7.   All DLCIs and DLCI number should be configured as shown in Figures B-19, B-20, B-21, and B-22.

Step 8.   Return to the main menu.

Step 9.   Use the down arrow to go down to Packet Manager (see Figure B-23).

Select **Packet Cncts** and press **Enter**.

Figure B-23   Select Packet Cncts

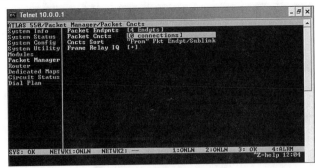

Step 10.   Configure Packet Cncts as shown (see Figure B-24).

Figure B-24   Configure Packet Cncts

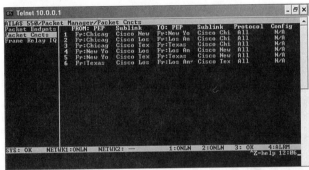

Step 11.   Return to the main menu.

Step 12.   Scroll down to **Dedicated Maps** (see Figure B-25).

Use the down arrow to scroll to **Create/Edit Maps** and press **Enter**.

Figure B-25   Select Create/Edit Maps

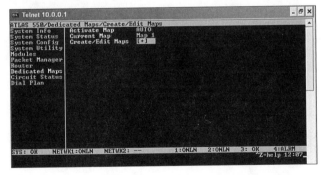

Step 13.   Use the right-arrow key and select **Connects** (see Figure B-26).

Figure B-26   Select Connects

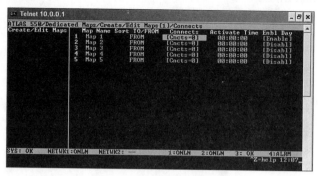

Step 14.   Configure each port as shown in Figure B-27.

Each of the four slots should be directed to a location as shown.

Figure B-27   Final Port Configuration

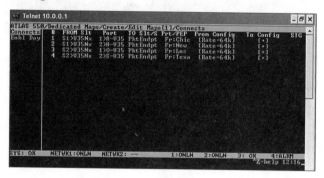

Note

To insert a new line, press the letter **I**.

To delete a line, press the letter **D**.

Return to the preceding screen.

Return to the main menu.

Router Interface Summary Chart

For most of the CCNA 4 labs, you need to examine the following chart to correctly reference the router interface identifiers to use in commands based on the equipment in your lab.

Router Model	Ethernet Interface 1	Ethernet Interface 2	Serial Interface 1	Serial Interface 2
800 (806)	Ethernet 0 (E0)	Ethernet 1 (E1)	—	—
1600	Ethernet 0 (E0)	Ethernet 1 (E1)	Serial 0 (S0)	Serial 1 (S1)
1700	FastEthernet 0 (FA0)	FastEthernet 1 (FA1)	Serial 0 (S0)	Serial 1 (S1)
2500	Ethernet 0 (E0)	Ethernet 1 (E1)	Serial 0 (S0)	Serial 1 (S1)
2600	FastEthernet 0/0 (FA0/0)	FastEthernet 0/1 (FA0/1)	Serial 0/0 (S0/0)	Serial 0/1 (S0/1)

To find out exactly how the router is configured, look at the interfaces to identify what type of and how many interfaces the router has. There is no way to effectively list all the combinations of configurations for each router class. The chart provides the identifiers for the possible combinations of interfaces in the device. This interface chart does not include any other type of interface, even though a specific router might contain one. An example of this is an ISDN BRI interface. The string in parentheses is the legal abbreviation that you can use in Cisco IOS Software commands to represent the interface.

Erasing and Reloading the Switch

For the majority of the labs in CCNA 4 focusing on switch configuration, it is necessary to start with a basic unconfigured switch; otherwise, the configuration parameters you enter might combine with previous ones and produce unpredictable results. The instructions here allow you to prepare the switch before performing the lab so that previous configuration options do not interfere with your configurations.

The following is the procedure for clearing out previous configurations and starting with an unconfigured switch. Instructions are provided for the 2900, 2950, and 1900 series switches.

2900 and 2950 Series Switches

Step 1. Disconnect the switch to be erased from all other switches. Verify that there is no uplink or backbone cabling to any other switch; otherwise, VLAN configuration information can be transferred automatically.

Step 2. Enter privileged EXEC mode by entering **enable**.

If prompted for a password, enter **class** (if that does not work, ask the instructor):

```
Switch> enable
```

Step 3. Remove the VLAN database information file.

```
Switch# delete flash:vlan.dat
Delete filename [vlan.dat]?[Enter]
Delete flash:vlan.dat? [confirm][Enter]
```

If there is no VLAN file, this message appears:

```
%Error deleting flash:vlan.dat (No such file or directory)
```

Step 4. Remove the switch startup configuration file from NVRAM.

```
Switch# erase startup-config
```

The responding line prompt will be this:

```
Erasing the nvram filesystem will remove all files! Continue? [confirm]
```

Press **Enter** to confirm.

The response should be this:

```
Erase of nvram: complete
```

Step 5. Check that VLAN information was deleted.

Verify that the VLAN configuration was deleted in Step 3 using the **show vlan** command. If previous VLAN configuration information (other than the default management VLAN 1) is still present, you must power-cycle the switch (hardware restart) instead of issuing the **reload** command. To power-cycle the switch, remove the power cord from the back of the switch or unplug it. Then plug it back in.

If the VLAN information was successfully deleted in Step 3, go to Step 6 and restart the switch using the **reload** command.

Step 6.   Software restart (using the **reload** command).

Note

This step is not necessary if the switch was restarted using the power-cycle method.

A. In privileged EXEC mode, enter the command **reload**.

```
Switch(config)# reload
```

The responding line prompt will be this:

```
System configuration has been modified. Save? [yes/no]:
```

B. Type **n** and then press **Enter**.

The responding line prompt will be this:

```
Proceed with reload? [confirm][Enter]
```

The first line of the response will be this:

```
Reload requested by console.
```

After the switch has reloaded, the line prompt will be this:

```
Would you like to enter the initial configuration dialog? [yes/no]:
```

C. Type **n** and then press **Enter**.

The responding line prompt will be this:

```
Press RETURN to get started![Enter]
```

1900 Series Switches

Step 1.   Remove VLAN Trunking Protocol (VTP) information.

```
#delete vtp
```

This command resets the switch with VTP parameters set to factory defaults. All other parameters will be unchanged.

```
Reset system with VTP parameters set to factory defaults, [Y]es or [N]o?
```

Type **y** and press **Enter**.

Step 2.   Remove the switch startup configuration from NVRAM.

```
#delete nvram
```

This command resets the switch with factory defaults. All system parameters will revert to their default factory settings. All static and dynamic addresses will be removed.

```
Reset system with factory defaults, [Y]es or [N]o?
```

Type **y** and press **Enter**.

Erasing and Reloading the Router

For some of the CCNA 4 labs, it is necessary to start with a basic unconfigured router; otherwise, the configuration parameters you enter might combine with previous ones and produce unpredictable results. The instructions here allow you to prepare the router before performing the lab so that previous configuration options do not interfere with your configurations.

The following is the procedure for clearing out previous configurations and starting with an unconfigured router.

Step 1. Enter privileged EXEC mode by entering **enable**.

```
Router> enable
```

If prompted for a password, enter **class**. (If that does not work, ask your instructor.)

Step 2. In privileged EXEC mode, enter the command **erase startup-config**.

```
Router# erase startup-config
```

The response from the router will be this:

```
Erasing the nvram filesystem will remove all files! Continue? [confirm]
```

Step 3. Press **Enter** to confirm.

The response will be this:

```
Erase of nvram: complete
```

Step 4. In privileged EXEC mode, enter the command **reload**.

```
Router# reload
response:
System configuration has been modified. Save? [yes/no]:
```

Type **n** and then press **Enter**.

The router responds with this:

```
Proceed with reload? [confirm]
```

Step 5. Press **Enter** to confirm.

The first line of the response will be this:

```
Reload requested by console.
```

After the router reloads, the prompt will be this:

```
Would you like to enter the initial configuration dialog? [yes/no]:
```

Step 6. Type **n** and then press **Enter**.

The responding prompt will be this:

```
Press RETURN to get started!
```

Step 7. Press **Enter**.

Now, the router is ready for you to perform the assigned lab.

Notes

Notes

Notes

Notes

Notes